Mediterranean Cooking

Mediterranean Cooking

**MORE THAN 150 FAVORITES
TO ENJOY WITH FAMILY AND FRIENDS**

STERLING

New York

Contents

Introduction 6
Snacks and Small Plates 14
Soups, Salads and Sides 64
Seafood 136
Poultry 196
Meat 234
Vegetarian 264
Sweets and Drinks 292
Glossary 354
Index 359

Introduction

For those who enjoy the Mediterranean lifestyle, food is a ritual—an experience that must be shared with family and friends. It is about love, spirituality and enjoying culinary traditions that date back thousands of years.

Of course it's hardly a surprise that Mediterranean cuisine inspires such joy. The region boasts ideal growing conditions for a wide variety of food and features an abundance of fresh vegetables. Eggplants, garlic, chickpeas, onions and tomatoes, for example, are used in many different types of dishes. The region is perhaps best known for the olive and lemon trees that dot the landscape as these trees provide a few of the most important ingredients in Mediterranean cooking.

And while there are many countries that lay claim to the coastline of the Mediterranean sea, if the region were to be loosely organized into three distinct areas, it would be comprised of southern Europe, Northern Africa and the eastern Mediterranean. Therefore, you'll find the recipes in this collection represent some of the best dishes from each area.

Not sure where to start? You may want to build a meal out of a variety of small plates that begin this book (in Greece, they're called *mezzes* and in Spain they're known as *tapas*). With everything from cheese-filled pastries to grilled shrimp or grape leaves that hold a tasty bite of rice and lamb, you'll find a variety of dishes that cater to everyone's personal preferences. These small plate dishes are usually shared by everyone at the table; unlike an appetizer, they are not intended to whet the appetite for the next course, but can be considered a meal in themselves. Of course they make for quite tasty snacks, too.

With so many people living in close proximity to the sea, it's also easy to see why seafood features prominently in the Mediterranean cuisine, and the variety of ways it can be prepared is amazing. Try the spicy fish tagine or the grilled salmon with chermoulla sauce if you like bold, enticing flavors. If your taste runs more mild, you might enjoy giving the baked fish with saffron, leek and potato a try. Many of the recipes include a simple salad or side as part of the meal, but there are plenty of other choices if you want to mix it up a bit.

Just don't skip dessert. You'll find a variety of sweet endings in the last chapter of this book. For a simple weeknight meal you might enjoy an easy-to-make rice pudding with cinnamon and vanilla or a colorful melon salad topped with citrus sugar. More lavish celebrations call for a smooth and creamy buttermilk custard topped with honeyed figs, or perhaps a pan of classic baklava. Whatever the occasion, this collection will inspire hospitality and help you enjoy every stage of the cooking process, for this food is more than just sustenance: it is a celebration of life.

Mediterranean essential ingredients

OLIVE OIL
Available in several grades, virgin oils are the best. Extra virgin and virgin oils are best used for salad oils and gentle frying of delicate foods. "Pure olive oil" (or simply "olive oil"), is usually a mixture of virgin and refined oil, and is best for general frying.

TAHINI
A sesame seed paste used in a variety of dips and sauces; it lends a rich, nutty flavor to finished dishes. It is available from health food stores, the health food section in most supermarkets and Middle Eastern food stores.

PHYLLO PASTRY
Paper-thin sheets of raw pastry; are used by brushing with oil or melted butter and stacking one on another, then cutting and folding as the recipe directs. This creates a layered, crackling-crisp, airy crust or wrapping for small pastries such as spanakopita.

GREEK-STYLE YOGURT
This yogurt has been strained in a cloth (traditionally muslin), to remove the whey and to give it a creamy consistency. It's ideal for use in dips and dressings and is widely available in most supermarkets.

FETA CHEESE

Traditionally made with sheep's milk, now most often cow's milk. It is shaped into large blocks which are salted, sliced and salted again, then packed in whey for a month or so. It ends up firm, sharp-flavored and salty. Packed in brine, it should be eaten within a day or two of purchase.

HALOUMI CHEESE

This Cypriot cheese is often used in Greek cooking. It's a firm, traditionally sheep-milk cheese (also goat's or cow's-milk varieties) with a minty, salty flavor; it does not break down when cooked, however it should be eaten while still warm as it becomes tough and rubbery on cooling.

SHERRY & SHERRY VINEGAR

A fortified wine made from white grapes grown near Jerez, Spain. Stored in American oak casks, it is aged in the solera system (where new wine is periodically added and moved progressively through a series of barrels). Sherry is aged this way for a minimum of 3 years; sherry vinegar from Jerez is aged this way for an average of 6 years.

MANCHEGO CHEESE

A famous semi-firm Spanish sheep's cheese which is mild when young, but after aging for 3 months or longer, becomes a rich golden color and develops a full, tangy flavor with the characteristic aftertaste of sheep's milk.

BELL PEPPER
Bell peppers belong to the same family as hot chilis, but do not contain heat. This heatless fruit is known as pimiento in Spain. Bell peppers are green when unripe, and ripen to red, yellow, purple-black or brown. Canned red ones are available, often imported under its Spanish name pimiento.

ORANGES
The most popular citrus fruit, oranges are available all year round. There are two main kinds of orange: sweet (navel, valencia, blood oranges) and bitter (seville). Oranges will keep well for a few days at room temperature; for longer storage, store in the refrigerator.

OLIVES
Olives are eaten green (unripe) and black (ripe). Both are inedibly bitter when picked and must be leached of their bitter juices by salt-curing or brining. Green olives are firm and tangy; available pitted, with pits or stuffed. Black olives are more mellow in flavor than green ones and are softer in texture; available stone-in, with pits and sliced.

CHICKPEAS (GARBANZO BEANS)
An irregularly round, sandy-colored legume used extensively in Mediterranean, Indian and Hispanic cooking. They have a firm texture even after cooking, a floury mouth-feel and robust nutty flavor. Available canned (pre-cooked) or dried (must be soaked in water for several hours before cooking).

CHORIZO

Are small, coarse-textured pork and beef sausages. They are deeply smoked, very spicy and dry-cured so that they do not need cooking. Serve chorizo cold with bread, pickled vegetables and a glass of sherry as a tapas dish, or grilled or fried and served hot. Chorizo can also be purchased as a fresh sausage.

SEAFOOD

With its extensive coastline, fresh seafood is an important element of Mediterranean cuisine. Fish, shrimp, mussels, clams, octopus and squid (to name just a few) are prominent, and commonly used in many classic dishes such as paella.

ALMONDS

Flat, pointy-tipped nut with a pitted brown shell; its creamy white kernel is covered by a brown skin. Mild in flavor when raw, roasting brings out a warm, embracing flavor. They are available in the shell, as whole kernels (raw or roasted), blanched (kernels, skins removed), flaked (paper-thin slices), slivered (pieces cut lengthways), and ground.

SARDINES & ANCHOVIES

Small oily fish. Sardines are commonly purchased canned (tightly packed in oil or brine); fresh sardines are also available and grilled, pickled or smoked. Anchovy fillets are preserved and packed in oil or salt in small cans or jars, and are strong in flavor. Fresh anchovies are much milder in flavor.

CINNAMON
Available in pieces (sticks or quills) and ground; it is one of the world's most common spices and is used as a sweet, fragrant flavoring. True cinnamon is the dried inner bark of the shoots of the Sri Lankan native cinnamon tree; it is often blended with cassia (chinese cinnamon) to produce "cinnamon" commonly found in supermarkets.

OREGANO
Dried Greek oregano is often sold in bunches. Store dried herbs away from heat or light in airtight packets or containers; do not store in the fridge as transferring between a cold fridge and a warm kitchen can cause condensation inside the packet and spoil its contents.

SAFFRON
The stigma (three per flower) of the saffron crocus. It imparts a yellow-orange color to food once infused—use with restraint as too much can overwhelm other flavors. Quality can vary greatly and the best is the most expensive spice in the world. Nearly three-quarters of the world's saffron production comes from Spain.

PAPRIKA
Paprika is made from the dried ground fruits of several members of the chili family. There are many grades and types available depending on the fruit from which it is made, including sweet, hot, mild and smoked. Paprika produced in Spain is particularly fine and is an important ingredient in romesco sauce.

SUMAC
A purple-red spice ground from the berries of a small Mediterranean shrub. Adds a tart, lemony flavor to dips and dressings and goes well with meat, chicken and fish, tomato and avocado.

SPLIT PEAS
These are available in both green and yellow varieties; they have a sweet, strong pea flavor. Best known for pea and ham soup, split peas can also be found in Middle Eastern soups and stews.

ZA'ATAR
This blend of roasted dried thyme, oregano, marjoram, sesame seeds and sumac is found in many Middle Eastern kitchens. Za'atar is traditionally sprinkled on toast spread with ricotta, or try it tossed with roasted potato wedges.

COUSCOUS
The staple cereal of North Africa, made from fine semolina. The minuscule pellets are steamed over the pot in which the meat and vegetables are cooking or, for sweet couscous, over water, then mixed with sugar, nuts and fruits.

Snacks and Small Plates

Thyme and garlic marinated olives

1 lemon
½ cup olive oil
2 cloves garlic, crushed
3 sprigs fresh thyme
1 bay leaf
2 cups large kalamata olives, rinsed, drained

1 Sterilize jar and lid (see tip).

2 Meanwhile, using a vegetable peeler, peel zest thinly from lemon, avoiding white pith. Combine zest, oil, garlic, thyme and bay leaf in medium saucepan over medium heat; heat until warm and garlic begins to sizzle. Add olives; cook over low heat 10 minutes.

3 Spoon hot olives into sterilized jar. Seal jar while hot.

prep + cook time 15 minutes (+ standing) **serves** 12

tip To sterilize jars: wash the jar and lid in warm soapy water; rinse well. Place jar in large saucepan and cover with water. Bring to a boil and boil for 10 minutes. Carefully drain water from jars; transfer jar and lid to a baking sheet lined with a clean tea towel. Cover with a sheet of foil and place in a 200°F oven until dry. Use straight from the oven.

Serve olives warm if you like or store olives in refrigerator for one week.

Olive and cheese fritters

    2 teaspoons dried yeast
    1 cup warm water
    2 cups all-purpose flour
    ½ teaspoon salt
    ¼ cup pitted black olives, coarsely chopped
    4 drained anchovy fillets, finely chopped
    4 sun-dried tomatoes, drained, finely chopped
    6 ounces bocconcini cheese, finely chopped
    1 small white onion, finely chopped
    2 cloves garlic, crushed
vegetable oil, for deep-frying

1 Combine yeast and the water in a measuring cup. Sift flour and salt into large bowl, gradually stir in yeast mixture to form a sticky, wet batter. Cover; stand in warm place about 1 hour or until doubled in size.

2 Stir olives, anchovy, tomato, cheese, onion and garlic into batter; season.

3 Heat oil in large saucepan; deep-fry heaped teaspoons of batter, in batches, about 3 minutes or until fritters are lightly browned and cooked through. Drain on paper towels; stand 2 minutes before serving.

prep + cook time 30 minutes (+ standing) **makes** 40

Chickpea patties with tahini sauce

1 can (15 ounces) chickpeas, rinsed, drained
½ small brown onion, chopped coarsely
1 egg
½ cup coarsely grated kasseri cheese
¼ cup coarsely chopped fresh oregano
1 clove garlic, crushed
1 tablespoon olive oil
½ cup stale breadcrumbs
2 tablespoons olive oil, extra

tahini sauce
2 tablespoons finely chopped fresh flat-leaf parsley
2 tablespoons tahini
2 tablespoons hot water
1 tablespoon olive oil
1 tablespoon lemon juice
1 clove garlic, crushed

1 Process chickpeas, onion, egg, cheese, oregano, garlic and olive oil until thick. Transfer to medium bowl; stir in breadcrumbs. Season to taste; stand 10 minutes.

2 Meanwhile, make tahini sauce.

3 With wet hands, shape level tablespoons of mixture into patties.

4 Heat extra oil in large frying pan; cook patties about 2 minutes each side or until browned. Drain on paper towels.

5 Serve patties with sauce.

tahini sauce Combine ingredients in small bowl; season to taste.

prep + cook time 30 minutes (+ standing) **makes** 22

Fava bean patties with minted yogurt

½ cup green split peas
1 pound frozen fava beans
1 onion, finely chopped
2 cloves garlic, crushed
⅓ cup all-purpose flour
¼ cup packaged breadcrumbs
1 egg
cooking-oil spray

minted yogurt
⅔ cup plain yogurt
¼ cup finely chopped fresh mint
1 teaspoon finely grated lime zest
2 tablespoons lime juice

1 Place peas in medium pan of boiling water; return to a boil. Reduce heat; simmer until tender. Drain.

2 Meanwhile, place beans in medium pan of boiling water; return to a boil. Drain. Cool in iced water; drain. Discard skin. Mash beans and peas together in large bowl; cool.

3 Stir onion, garlic, flour, breadcrumbs and egg into bean mixture; season to taste. Using hands, shape mixture into eight patties; place on baking sheet lined with parchment paper. Refrigerate 30 minutes.

4 Meanwhile, make minted yogurt.

5 Lightly spray heated large skillet with oil; cook patties, in batches, until browned and heated through. Remove from pan.

6 Serve patties with minted yogurt.

minted yogurt Combine ingredients in small bowl; season to taste.

prep + cook time 40 minutes (+ refrigeration) **serves** 4

Paella croquettes

1 cup long-grain white rice
2 cups chicken stock
1 dried bay leaf
1 teaspoon ground turmeric
2 teaspoons olive oil
1 clove garlic, crushed
1 red onion, coarsely chopped
1 chorizo sausage (5 ounces), coarsely chopped
¼ pound smoked chicken, coarsely chopped
1 tablespoon finely chopped fresh flat-leaf parsley
¼ cup all-purpose flour
2 eggs, lightly beaten
1 tablespoon milk
1 cup packaged breadcrumbs
vegetable oil, for deep-frying

1 Combine rice, stock, bay leaf and turmeric in medium saucepan; bring to a boil, stirring. Reduce heat; simmer, covered, about 12 minutes or until rice is tender. Remove from heat; stand, covered, 10 minutes. Fluff rice with fork, discard bay leaf; cool.

2 Meanwhile, heat olive oil in large frying pan; cook garlic, onion and chorizo, stirring, until onion softens; cool.

3 Blend or process rice, chorizo mixture, chicken and parsley until ingredients come together; season to taste. With wet hands, shape ¼ cups of rice mixture into croquettes. Toss croquettes in flour; shake off excess. Dip in combined eggs and milk, then in breadcrumbs. Place croquettes on baking sheet lined with parchment paper; cover, refrigerate 30 minutes.

4 Heat vegetable oil in large saucepan; deep-fry croquettes, in batches, until lightly browned.

prep + cook time 50 minutes (+ cooling & refrigeration) **makes** 12

Deep-fried eggplant with fresh herb sauce

2 eggplant (about 1 pound)
2 tablespoons all-purpose flour
vegetable oil, for deep-frying

fresh herb sauce
1 cup each loosely packed fresh oregano and flat-leaf parsley
⅓ cup olive oil
2 cloves garlic, crushed
1 teaspoon finely grated lemon zest
1 tablespoon lemon juice

1 Make fresh herb sauce.

2 Cut each eggplant into 10 slices. Season flour with salt and pepper. Toss eggplant in flour, shake away excess.

3 Heat vegetable oil in medium saucepan or wok. Deep-fry eggplant, in batches, until browned and tender. Remove from pan; drain on paper towels.

4 Serve eggplant drizzled with sauce.

fresh herb sauce Process ingredients until smooth; season to taste.

prep + cook time 20 minutes **makes** 20 slices

tip Store sauce in airtight container in refrigerator.

27

Sardine dip

6 ounces light cream cheese, softened
2 tablespoons lemon juice
few drops Tabasco sauce
1 can (3½ ounces) sardines in spring water, drained, mashed
1 shallot, finely chopped
2 teaspoons finely chopped fresh flat-leaf parsley
¼ teaspoon cracked black pepper

1 Beat cream cheese, juice and sauce in small bowl with electric mixer until smooth.

2 Stir in remaining ingredients until combined; season to taste.

prep time 10 minutes **makes** 1 cup

serving suggestion Sprinkle with extra finely chopped fresh flat-leaf parsley; serve with crusty bread or crackers.

Skordalia

3 medium potatoes (about 1 pound), unpeeled
3 cloves garlic
½ teaspoon salt
½ cup olive oil
¼ cup lemon juice
½ cup milk

1 Boil, steam or microwave potatoes until tender. Drain.

2 Meanwhile, pound garlic and salt in a mortar and pestle until smooth, or, chop the garlic and salt together on a board and use the flat side of the knife blade to press garlic into a paste.

3 When potatoes are cool enough to handle, halve and spoon out flesh. Push flesh through sieve into large bowl. Whisk in oil, juice and garlic mixture then milk. Season with salt and white pepper.

prep + cook time 40 minutes **makes** 3 cups

tip We used russet potatoes, also known as Idaho.

serving suggestions Pita bread and raw vegetable sticks.

Tomato and feta toasts

1 small loaf French bread
2 tablespoons olive oil
1 clove garlic, peeled, halved
3 small ripe tomatoes, finely chopped
2 ounces feta cheese, crumbled
1 tablespoon fresh oregano

1 Preheat oven to 340°F (325° convection).

2 Cut bread on the diagonal into four thick slices; split slices. Brush bread with half the oil. Place on baking sheet. Toast in oven about 20 minutes, turning bread halfway, or until crisp. Rub toasts with garlic.

3 Season tomato; spoon onto toasts. Stand 20 minutes.

4 Top tomato with cheese; drizzle with remaining oil. Sprinkle with oregano.

prep + cook time 35 minutes (+ standing) **makes** 8

tip This dish is very simple. Success lies in the quality of the ingredients: choose ripe tomatoes, good bread and a quality oil.

Artichoke spinach dip

1 jar (11 ounces) marinated artichokes, drained
½ pound frozen chopped spinach, thawed
½ cup sour cream
¼ cup mayonnaise
¾ cup coarsely grated Pecorino romano cheese
1 clove garlic, crushed

1 Preheat oven to 400°F (375°F convection).

2 Chop artichokes coarsely. Combine artichokes with remaining ingredients in medium bowl. Transfer mixture to 2-cup oven-proof dish.

3 Cook dip, covered, 20 minutes.

prep + cook time 30 minutes **makes** 2 cups

SNACKS AND SMALL PLATES

Eggplant dip

2 large eggplants (about 2 pounds)
½ cup olive oil
6 tomatoes
3 cloves garlic, crushed
⅓ cup each coarsely chopped fresh flat-leaf parsley and cilantro
1 teaspoon ground cumin

1 Preheat oven to 400°F (375°F convection).

2 Pierce eggplants all over with fork or skewer. Place eggplants on oiled baking sheet; drizzle with 2 tablespoons of the oil. Roast eggplants, uncovered, about 50 minutes or until softened.

3 Meanwhile, place tomatoes on another oiled baking sheet; drizzle with 2 tablespoons of the oil. Roast tomatoes for last 15 minutes of eggplant cooking time. Cool 20 minutes.

4 When cool enough to handle, peel eggplants and tomatoes; discard skin. Seed tomatoes; chop tomato and eggplant coarsely.

5 Heat remaining oil in large skillet; cook garlic, eggplant and tomato, stirring occasionally, about 20 minutes or until thick. Add herbs; cook, stirring, 5 minutes. Transfer mixture to medium bowl, stir in cumin; cool 20 minutes. Season to taste. Serve with crusty bread.

prep + cook time 1 hour 20 minutes (+ cooling) **makes** 3 cups

White bean dip with pita crisps

1   clove garlic, crushed
¼   cup lightly packed fresh flat-leaf parsley leaves
1   can (15 ounces) white beans, rinsed, drained
1   teaspoon ground cumin
⅓   cup olive oil
6   pita bread, cut into sixths

1 Preheat the oven to 400°F (375°F convection).

2 Blend or process garlic, parsley, beans and cumin until combined. With the motor operating, add oil in a thin, steady stream until mixture is smooth.

3 Place pita on oiled baking sheets; bake 8 minutes or until lightly browned.

4 Serve dip with pita crisps and green olives.

prep + cook time 20 minutes **serves** 8

tip This recipe can be made a day ahead. Store pita crisps in an airtight container.

Goat cheese with chickpeas and bell peppers

2 large green bell peppers
2 large red bell peppers
2 tablespoons olive oil
1 red onion, thinly sliced
2 cloves garlic, crushed
1 teaspoon ground cumin
½ teaspoon hot paprika
1 can (15 ounces) chickpeas, rinsed, drained
2 teaspoons fresh lemon zest
1 tablespoon lemon juice
⅓ cup coarsely chopped fresh flat-leaf parsley
2 ounces soft goat cheese

1 Preheat oven to 400°F (375°F convection). Oil baking sheets.

2 Quarter bell peppers; discard seeds and membranes. Roast, skin-side up, until skin blisters and blackens. Cover bell peppers with plastic or paper for 5 minutes; peel away skin, then slice bell peppers thinly.

3 Heat oil in large skillet; stir onion and garlic, until onion softens. Add spices and half the chickpeas; cook, stirring, about 2 minutes or until fragrant. Add bell peppers; cook, stirring, until heated through. Remove from heat; stir in zest, juice and parsley. Cool.

4 Meanwhile, coarsely mash remaining chickpeas with cheese in medium bowl.

5 Stir bell pepper mixture into cheese mixture; season to taste. Serve dip with soft bread rolls or toasted pita bread.

prep + cook time 50 minutes **makes** 3 cups

Dolmades

2 tablespoons olive oil
2 onions, finely chopped
¼ pound lean ground lamb
¾ cup white long-grain rice
2 tablespoons pine nuts
½ cup finely chopped fresh flat-leaf parsley
2 tablespoons each finely chopped fresh dill and mint
¼ cup lemon juice
2 cups water
1 pound preserved grape leaves
¾ cup yogurt

1 Heat oil in large saucepan; cook onion, stirring, until softened. Add lamb; cook, stirring, until browned. Stir in rice and pine nuts. Add herbs, 2 tablespoons of the juice and half the water; bring to a boil. Reduce heat; simmer, covered, 10 minutes or until water is absorbed and rice is partially cooked. Cool.

2 Rinse grape leaves in cold water. Drop leaves into a large pot of boiling water, in batches, for a few seconds, transfer to colander; rinse under cold water, drain well.

3 Place a grape leaf, smooth-side down on work surface, trim large stem. Place a heaped teaspoon of rice mixture in center. Fold stem end and sides over filling; roll up firmly. Line medium heavy-bottom saucepan with a few grape leaves; place rolls, close together, seam-side down, on leaves.

4 Pour over the remaining water; cover rolls with any remaining leaves. Place a plate on top of leaves to weigh down rolls. Cover pan tightly, bring to a boil. Reduce heat; simmer, over very low heat, 1½ hours. Remove from heat; stand, covered, about 2 hours or until liquid has been absorbed.

5 Serve dolmades with combined yogurt and remaining juice.

prep + cook time 3 hours (+ standing) **serves** 10

tip Preserved grape leaves are packed in brine so should be rinsed and dried before use. Fresh leaves should be softened in boiling water for a minute until pliable, then dried.

Cheese phyllo triangles

1 cup cottage cheese

3 ounces feta cheese

1 egg

2 tablespoons each finely chopped fresh oregano and flat-leaf parsley

15 sheets frozen phyllo pastry, thawed

¼ cup olive oil

1 Preheat oven to 425°F (400°F convection). Oil baking sheets; line with parchment paper.

2 Combine cheeses, egg and herbs in medium bowl; season with pepper.

3 Brush 1 sheet of pasty with some of the oil; top with 2 more sheets, brushing each with more oil. Cut layered sheets into 3 strips lengthways. Place 1 level tablespoon of cheese mixture at one narrow edge of each pastry strip. Fold one corner of pastry diagonally over filling to form a triangle. Continue folding to end of strip, retaining triangular shape. Repeat to make 15 triangles in total.

4 Place triangles, seam-side down, on baking sheets; brush with a little more oil. Bake triangles about 15 minutes or until browned lightly.

prep + cook time 30 minutes **makes** 15

tip When working with the first three sheets of pastry, cover remaining pastry with a sheet of parchment paper then a damp tea towel to prevent it from drying out.

Feta and artichoke pizzetta

1 small pizza crust (8 inches in diameter)
2 ounces feta cheese, crumbled
1 teaspoon olive oil
1 marinated artichoke, thinly sliced
1 tablespoon fresh oregano leaves
2 teaspoons lemon juice

1 Preheat oven to 425°F (400°F convection). Place pizza crust on baking sheet.

2 Combine 1 tablespoon of the cheese with oil. Spread pizza base with cheese paste; top with artichoke then sprinkle with remaining cheese.

3 Bake about 8 minutes.

4 Serve pizzetta sprinkled with oregano and juice.

prep + cook time 15 minutes **makes** 1

tip Double or quadruple the recipe depending on how many you wish to serve. Look for marinated artichokes in the olive bar section of your grocery store.

Sardines with caper and parsley topping

8 sardines, cleaned
⅓ cup self-rising flour
½ teaspoon sweet paprika
olive oil, for shallow-frying

caper and parsley topping
2 tablespoons rinsed, drained baby capers, finely chopped
1 clove garlic, crushed
¼ cup finely chopped fresh flat-leaf parsley
2 teaspoons fresh lemon zest
2 teaspoons lemon juice

1 Make caper and parsley topping.

2 To butterfly sardines, cut through the underside of the fish to the tail. Break backbone at tail; peel away backbone. Trim sardines.

3 Coat fish in combined flour and paprika; shake away excess. Heat oil in large skillet; shallow-fry fish, in batches, until cooked through, drain on paper towels.

4 Sprinkle fish with caper and parsley topping. Serve with lemon wedges, if desired.

caper and parsley topping Combine ingredients in small bowl.

prep + cook time 45 minutes **serves** 8

tip The caper and parsley topping is best made on the day of serving; store, covered, in the refrigerator until ready to use.

Deep-fried baby calamari

1   pound baby calamari, frozen, thawed
⅓ cup all-purpose flour
vegetable oil, for deep-frying
2   teaspoons dried oregano

1 Slice calamari into thin rings. Season flour with salt and pepper.

2 Heat oil in medium saucepan or wok. Toss calamari in flour mixture; shake away excess. Deep-fry calamari, in batches, until browned lightly and tender. Drain on paper towels. Sprinkle with oregano; serve with a squeeze of lemon juice.

prep + cook time 15 minutes **serves** 4

tip Don't overcook the calamari or it will toughen. It should take about 30 seconds to cook one small batch at a time. Reheat the oil before frying the next batch of calamari.

serving suggestion Lemon wedges.

Saganaki shrimp

1 tablespoon olive oil
1 white onion, finely chopped
4 cloves garlic, crushed
1 can (14 ounces) crushed tomatoes
¾ cup dry white wine
2 pounds uncooked large shrimp
¼ cup each coarsely chopped fresh flat-leaf parsley and fresh oregano
6 ounces feta cheese, crumbled

1 Heat oil in large oven-proof skillet; cook onion and garlic, stirring, until onion softens. Add tomatoes and wine; bring to a boil. Reduce heat; simmer, covered, 10 minutes, stirring occasionally.

2 Meanwhile, shell and devein shrimp, leaving tails intact.

3 Add shrimp and herbs to tomato mixture; simmer, covered, 10 minutes, stirring occasionally.

4 Meanwhile, preheat broiler.

5 Sprinkle cheese over shrimp mixture; place under broiler until cheese browns lightly.

prep + cook time 45 minutes **serves** 4

tip "Saganaki," meaning little frying pan in Greek, refers today to a number of dishes cooked in a single skillet.

Mini chicken souvlaki

2 pounds chicken thighs, boneless, skinless
2 tablespoons olive oil
2 tablespoons lemon juice
⅓ cup finely chopped fresh mint
2 cloves garlic, crushed
1½ teaspoons smoked paprika

1 Trim any fat from chicken; cut into ¾-inch thick strips. Combine chicken with remaining ingredients in medium bowl. Thread chicken onto 20 bamboo skewers. Cover; refrigerate 3 hours or overnight.

2 Cook skewers in heated oiled grill pan until browned and cooked through.

prep + cook time 35 minutes (+ refrigeration) **makes** 20

tip Soak bamboo skewers in cold water for at least an hour before using to prevent them from scorching during cooking. For optimum flavor, marinate the chicken overnight.

serving suggestion Lemon wedges.

Beef and fig cigars

2 tablespoons butter
1 onion, finely chopped
½ teaspoon ground cinnamon
2 cloves garlic, crushed
½ pound lean ground beef
¾ cup finely chopped dried figs
1 tablespoon finely chopped fresh chives
8 sheets frozen phyllo pastry, thawed
cooking-oil spray
½ cup plum sauce

1 Melt butter in large skillet; cook onion, cinnamon and garlic, stirring, until onion softens. Add beef; cook, stirring, until browned. Stir in figs and chives; cool 10 minutes.

2 Meanwhile, preheat oven to 400°F (375°F convection). Coat two baking sheets with cooking oil spray.

3 Coat 1 pastry sheet with oil spray; cover with a second pastry sheet. Cut lengthways into three even strips, then crossways into four strips.

4 Place 1 rounded teaspoon of beef mixture along bottom of one narrow edge of a pastry strip, leaving ½-inch border. Fold narrow edge over beef mixture then fold in long sides; roll to enclose filling. Place cigar, seam-side down, on trays. Repeat process with remaining pastry and beef mixture.

5 Lightly spray cigars with oil. Bake about 10 minutes or until lightly browned. Serve with plum sauce.

prep + cook time 1 hour **makes** 48

tip Keep a plastic spray bottle filled with olive oil in the fridge and bring it to room temperature before using it to spray the phyllo. When working with the first two phyllo sheets, be sure to cover the remaining sheets with parchment paper then a damp tea towel to prevent them drying out.

Spiced meatballs with romesco sauce

½ pound chorizo sausages, coarsely chopped
1 small red onion, coarsely chopped
2 cloves garlic, crushed
1 pound lean ground beef
½ teaspoon ground nutmeg
1 tablespoon dry sherry
½ cup stale breadcrumbs
olive oil, for shallow-frying

romesco sauce
1 teaspoon dried red pepper flakes
2 cloves garlic, crushed
1 tablespoon slivered almonds, toasted
2 tomatoes, coarsely chopped
¼ cup extra virgin olive oil
1 tablespoon red wine vinegar

1 Make romesco sauce.

2 Blend or process chorizo, onion and garlic, pulsing until ingredients are finely chopped and combined. Transfer mixture to large bowl; stir in beef, nutmeg, sherry and breadcrumbs, season. Roll level tablespoons of mixture into balls.

3 Heat oil in large skillet; shallow-fry meatballs, in batches, until browned and cooked through. Drain on paper towels.

4 Serve meatballs with romesco sauce.

romesco sauce Soak red pepper flakes in hot water for 5 minutes; drain. Blend or process pepper flakes, garlic, nuts and tomato until smooth. With motor operating, gradually add combined oil and vinegar in thin steady stream until sauce is smooth.

prep + cook time 40 minutes **makes** 40

tip Meatballs and sauce can be made a day ahead. To reheat the meatballs, place them in a single layer, on baking sheet; cover with foil and make several slashes in the foil to allow steam to escape. Bake in oven preheated to 350°F (325°F convection) for about 20 minutes.

Meatballs in tomato sauce

½ pound lean ground beef
¼ pound ground pork
1 small onion, finely chopped
½ cup grated Pecorino romano cheese
½ cup stale breadcrumbs
¼ cup finely chopped fresh flat-leaf parsley
1 egg
5 cloves garlic, crushed
1 teaspoon ground cumin
2 tablespoons olive oil
1 onion, finely chopped
1 can (14 ounces) diced tomatoes

1 Combine beef, pork, onion, cheese, breadcrumbs, parsley, egg, 2 cloves garlic and cumin in medium bowl; season. Roll level tablespoons of mixture into balls.

2 Heat oil in large, non-stick skillet over medium-high heat; cook meatballs, in batches, until browned. Remove from skillet.

3 Cook onion in same pan, stirring, until softened. Stir in remaining garlic; cook until fragrant. Add tomatoes; return meatballs to skillet. Bring to a boil; simmer, uncovered, about 10 minutes or until meatballs are cooked through. Season to taste.

prep + cook time 35 minutes **makes** 24

tip To shape the meatballs, it's important to chop the onion finely. The secret to round meatballs is to make a circular movement with the skillet to roll the meatballs while they cook. Use ¾ pound ground meatloaf mix in place of ground beef and pork, if desired.

serving suggestion Crusty bread.

Chorizo cones with salsa

  1 can (15 ounces) refried beans
  1 tablespoon water
  2 chorizo sausages (5 ounces each), finely chopped
  ½ red bell pepper, finely chopped
  3 scallions, finely chopped
10 large (8-inch) flour tortillas, quartered
vegetable oil, for deep-frying

chili tomato salsa
  1 can (14 ounces) tomatoes
  2 fresh small red Thai chilies, seeded, quartered
  1 clove garlic, quartered
  ⅓ cup loosely packed fresh cilantro leaves
  1 small onion, quartered

1 Heat beans with the water in small saucepan.

2 Meanwhile, cook chorizo in large non-stick skillet, stirring, until crisp; drain on paper towels.

3 Combine bean mixture and chorizo in medium bowl with bell peppers and scallion; season to taste. Divide filling among tortilla pieces; roll each tortilla around filling into cone shape, secure with toothpick

4 Heat oil in large saucepan; deep-fry cones, in batches, until browned lightly and crisp. Drain on paper towels. Remove toothpicks.

5 Make salsa.

6 Serve hot cones with salsa.

salsa Blend or process ingredients until just combined.

prep + cook time 55 minutes **makes** 40

tip Chorizo filling and chili tomato salsa can be made a day ahead. Cover separately; refrigerate until required.

You need 40 toothpicks with points at each end for this recipe.

Soups, Salads and Sides

Lentil soup

  1 tablespoon olive oil
  1 onion, finely chopped
  2 cloves garlic, crushed
  1 cup brown lentils, rinsed, drained
  1 can (14 ounces) diced tomatoes
1½ cups chicken stock
1½ cups water
  1 bay leaf
  2 tablespoons coarsely chopped fresh dill

1 Heat oil in large saucepan; cook onion, stirring, until softened. Stir in garlic; cook until fragrant.

2 Stir in lentils, undrained tomatoes, stock, the water and bay leaf; bring to a boil. Reduce heat; simmer, covered, about 50 minutes or until lentils are tender. Season to taste. Discard bay leaf.

3 Serve soup sprinkled with dill.

prep + cook time 1 hour **serves** 4

serving suggestions A dash of red wine vinegar for each bowl and crusty bread.

Turnip soup

1 tablespoon olive oil
1 large onion, coarsely chopped
2 cloves garlic, crushed
2 teaspoons each cumin seeds and ground coriander
½ teaspoon hot paprika
3 pounds turnips, trimmed, coarsely chopped
6 cups chicken stock
½ cup heavy cream
⅓ cup coarsely chopped fresh flat-leaf parsley

1 Heat oil in large saucepan; cook onion and garlic, stirring, until onion softens. Add spices; cook, stirring, until fragrant.

2 Add turnip and stock to pan; bring to a boil. Reduce heat; simmer, uncovered, until turnips are tender. Cool 15 minutes.

3 Blend or process soup, in batches, until smooth. Return to same pan with cream; stir until hot.

4 Serve bowls of soup sprinkled with parsley.

prep + cook time 50 minutes **serves** 4

Cream of roasted garlic and potato soup

2 heads of garlic, unpeeled
2 tablespoons olive oil
2 onions, coarsely chopped
1 tablespoon fresh thyme
5 potatoes, coarsely chopped
5 cups chicken stock
¾ cup heavy cream

1 Preheat oven to 350°F (325°F convection).

2 Separate garlic into cloves; place unpeeled cloves, in single layer, on baking sheet. Drizzle with half the oil. Roast about 15 minutes or until garlic is soft. When cool enough to handle, squeeze garlic into small bowl, discard skins.

3 Meanwhile, heat remaining oil in large saucepan; cook onion and thyme, stirring, until onion softens. Add potato; cook, stirring, 5 minutes. Add stock; bring to a boil. Reduce heat; simmer, uncovered, about 15 minutes or until potato is tender. Stir in garlic; simmer, uncovered, 5 minutes.

4 Blend or process soup (or pass through a food mill or fine sieve), in batches, until smooth, then return to pan. Reheat until hot then stir in cream; season to taste. Divide soup among serving bowls; sprinkle with extra thyme, if desired.

prep + cook time 40 minutes **serves** 4

tip Garlic's cooking times make a huge difference to its pungency: the longer it's cooked, the more creamy in texture and subtly nutty in flavor it becomes.

Cream of spinach soup with lemon feta toast

3 tablespoons butter
1 large onion, finely chopped
2 cloves garlic, crushed
3 potatoes, coarsely chopped
3 cups chicken stock
4 cups water
2 pounds spinach, trimmed, coarsely chopped
¾ cup heavy cream

lemon feta toast
5 ounces feta cheese
2 teaspoons fresh lemon zest
1 small loaf French bread

1 Melt butter in large pot; cook onion and garlic, stirring, until onion softens. Add potato, stock and the water; bring to a boil. Reduce heat; simmer, covered, about 15 minutes or until potato is tender. Stir in spinach; cool 15 minutes.

2 Meanwhile, make lemon feta toast.

3 Blend or process soup, in batches, until smooth. Return soup to same cleaned pan, add cream; stir over medium heat until hot.

4 Serve bowls of soup with toast.

lemon feta toast Preheat broiler. Combine cheese with half the zest. Cut bread into ½-inch slices; discard end pieces. Toast slices one side; turn, sprinkle each slice with cheese mixture and remaining zest. Toast until lightly browned.

prep + cook time 55 minutes (+ cooling) **serves** 6

Chickpea, garlic and mint soup

2 teaspoons olive oil
2 onions, coarsely chopped
5 cloves garlic, crushed
1 teaspoon ground cumin
8 cups chicken stock
2 tablespoons white wine vinegar
2 cans (15 ounces) chickpeas, rinsed, drained
2 large tomatoes, seeded, finely chopped
2 tablespoons finely shredded fresh mint

1 Heat oil in large pot; cook onion and garlic, stirring, until softened. Add cumin; cook, stirring, until fragrant. Add stock and vinegar; bring to a boil. Add chickpeas; simmer, uncovered, 15 minutes.

2 Add tomato; simmer, uncovered, about 5 minutes or until tomato is soft. Season to taste.

3 Serve soup sprinkled with mint.

prep + cook time 35 minutes **serves** 6
serving suggestion Crusty white bread.

Chickpea tomato stew

2 tablespoons olive oil
2 onions, thinly sliced
1 tablespoon light brown sugar
2 teaspoons cumin seeds
1 teaspoon ground coriander
1 can (28 ounces) whole tomatoes
1 cup vegetable stock
2 cans (15 ounces) chickpeas, rinsed, drained
1 cup raisins
⅓ cup coarsely chopped preserved lemon zest
4 cups baby spinach leaves

1 Heat oil in large saucepan; cook onion and sugar over low heat, stirring occasionally, about 15 minutes or until onions are lightly caramelized. Add spices; cook, stirring, about 1 minute or until mixture is fragrant.

2 Add undrained tomatoes, stock, chickpeas, raisins and lemon; bring to a boil. Reduce heat; simmer, covered, about 30 minutes or until slightly thickened. Stir in spinach; season to taste.

prep + cook time 1 hour **serves** 6

Seafood soup

1 tablespoon olive oil
3 slices bacon, thinly sliced
1 onion, finely chopped
1 small fennel bulb, thinly sliced
3 cloves garlic, thinly sliced
2 tomatoes, seeded, coarsely chopped
2 tablespoons tomato paste
1 teaspoon hot paprika
½ cup dry white wine
1 can (28 ounces) whole tomatoes
3 cups fish stock
4 cups water
1 pound fingerling potatoes, cut into 1-inch pieces
2½ pounds frozen chopped seafood mix, thawed
½ cup coarsely chopped fresh flat-leaf parsley

1 Heat oil in large pot; cook bacon, stirring, until crisp. Drain on paper towels.

2 Add onion, fennel and garlic to pot; cook, stirring, until vegetables soften. Add fresh tomato; cook, stirring, until soft. Add tomato paste and paprika; cook, stirring, 2 minutes. Return bacon to pan with wine; cook, stirring, 2 minutes.

3 Slice canned tomatoes thickly, then add with juice from can to pan; add stock, the water and potato. Bring to a boil. Reduce heat; simmer, covered, about 20 minutes or until potato is tender.

4 Add seafood mix; cook, covered, about 3 minutes or until seafood is cooked. Season to taste; stir in parsley.

prep + cook time 50 minutes **serves** 6

tip We used a marinara mix with mussels in their shells.

Greek chicken and vegetable soup

1 whole chicken (about 3–4 pounds)
1 onion, halved
1 stalk celery, trimmed, coarsely chopped
14 cups water
¼ cup olive oil
1 onion, coarsely chopped
4 roma egg tomatoes, coarsely chopped
1 large potato, coarsely chopped
2 carrots, coarsely chopped
3 stalks celery, trimmed, coarsely chopped
3 bay leaves
1 large zucchini, coarsely chopped
½ cup small tube pasta, such as ditalini

1 Place chicken in large stockpot with halved onion, celery and the water; season. Bring to a boil. Reduce heat; simmer, uncovered, 45 minutes. Skim the surface of any froth; discard.

2 Remove chicken from stock; cool 10 minutes. Discard chicken skin and bones; chop chicken coarsely. Strain stock; discard solids. Wipe clean the stockpot.

3 Heat oil in large stockpot; cook chopped onion, stirring, until softened. Add tomato; cook, stirring, 3 minutes. Add potato, carrot, extra celery, bay leaves and strained stock; bring to the boil. Reduce heat; simmer, uncovered, 15 minutes.

4 Return chicken to stockpot with zucchini and pasta; simmer, uncovered, about 15 minutes or until pasta is tender. Season to taste.

prep + cook time 2 hours (+ cooling) **serves** 8
serving suggestion Crusty bread.

Chicken, lemon and rice soup

2 teaspoons olive oil
1 small onion, finely chopped
4 cups chicken stock
2 boneless, skinless chicken breasts, coarsely chopped
⅓ cup arborio rice
2 eggs
⅓ cup lemon juice
2 tablespoons finely chopped fresh flat-leaf parsley

1 Heat oil in large pot; cook onion, stirring, until it softens. Add stock, chicken and rice; bring to a boil. Reduce heat; simmer, covered, about 20 minutes or until rice is tender. Remove from heat.

2 Whisk eggs and juice in small bowl until smooth. Gradually whisk ½ cup hot soup into egg mixture, then stir warmed egg mixture back into soup.

3 Serve bowls of soup sprinkled with parsley.

prep + cook time 45 minutes **serves** 4

tip This soup is our take on the classic avgolemono (which translates as egg and lemon). There are as many variations of this soup as there are Greek families, but the avgolemono mixture, added near the end of the cooking time, is always the crowning glory.

Arborio rice is an excellent choice for this recipe due to its high starch level, making for a deliciously creamy soup.

Shredded beef soup

1 pound beef skirt steak
8 cups water
1 dried bay leaf
6 black peppercorns
1 large carrot, coarsely chopped
1 stalk celery, trimmed, coarsely chopped
1 tablespoon olive oil
1 onion, thickly sliced
1 red bell pepper, thickly sliced
1 green bell pepper, thickly sliced
2 cloves garlic, crushed
2 fresh long red chilies, finely chopped
1 teaspoon ground cumin
1 can (14 ounces) crushed tomatoes
⅓ cup loosely packed fresh oregano
1 trimmed corn cob

1 Tie beef with kitchen string at 1-inch intervals. Place in large pot with the water, bay leaf, peppercorns, carrot and celery; bring to a boil. Reduce heat; simmer, covered, 1½ hours. Uncover; simmer about 30 minutes or until beef is tender. Cool beef in stock 10 minutes.

2 Transfer beef to large bowl; using two forks, shred beef coarsely. Strain stock through sieve lined with cheesecloth over another large heatproof bowl; discard solids.

3 Heat oil in same cleaned pan; cook onion, bell peppers, garlic, chilies and cumin, stirring, until vegetables soften. Return beef and stock to pan with undrained tomatoes and ¼ cup of the oregano; bring to a boil. Reduce heat; simmer, uncovered, 10 minutes.

4 Cut corn kernels from cob. Add corn to soup; cook, uncovered, until just tender. Season to taste.

5 Serve soup sprinkled with remaining oregano.

prep + cook time 2 hours 40 minutes **serves** 4
serving suggestion Toasted flour tortillas.

Winter soup with oxtail and chickpeas

2 tablespoons olive oil
2 pounds oxtails, coarsely chopped
4 carrots, finely chopped
1 small leek, thinly sliced
4 cloves garlic, thinly sliced
2 stalks celery, trimmed, finely chopped
¼ cup tomato paste
3 dried bay leaves
8 cups beef stock
1 chorizo sausage (5 ounces), finely chopped
1 can (15 ounces) chickpeas, rinsed, drained
½ cup risoni pasta

1 Heat oil in large pot; cook oxtail, in batches, stirring until browned. Remove from pot.

2 Cook carrot, leek, garlic and celery in same pot, stirring, until leek softens. Return oxtail to pot with paste, bay leaves and stock; bring to a boil. Reduce heat; simmer, uncovered, about 3 hours or until meat is tender. Strain soup into large heatproof bowl. Remove meat from oxtail, shred coarsely; discard bones. Return meat and vegetable mixture to soup in bowl; cool. Cover; refrigerate overnight.

3 Remove fat from surface of soup, return soup to cleaned pot; bring to a boil.

4 Meanwhile, cook chorizo in small heated skillet, stirring, until crisp. Drain on paper towels.

5 Add chickpeas and pasta to soup; simmer, covered, about 8 minutes or until pasta is tender. Season to taste. Serve soup topped with chorizo.

prep + cook time 3 hours 30 minutes (+ refrigeration) **serves** 6

tip Oxtail is a very fatty cut of meat; this soup must be made a day ahead and refrigerated overnight to remove the excess fat which will solidify on the soup surface after refrigeration. This can simply be scraped off using a large spoon or ladle.

Pickled zucchini salad

4   zucchini (about a pound)
½   cup fresh dill sprigs
1   tablespoon fresh lemon zest

pickling liquid
¼   cup white wine vinegar
2   teaspoons sugar
1   teaspoon salt
1   tablespoon olive oil

1 Using vegetable peeler, slice zucchini lengthways into ribbons. Combine zucchini, dill and zest in heatproof bowl.

2 Make pickling liquid; pour hot liquid over zucchini mixture. Cool.

pickling liquid Stir vinegar, sugar and salt in small saucepan over medium heat until sugar dissolves; bring to a boil. Remove from heat; stir in oil.

prep + cook time 15 minutes (+ cooling) **serves** 4 as a side

Sweet cucumber and orange salad

2 large oranges
1 English cucumber
2 cups loosely packed fresh mint

honey lemon dressing
¼ cup avocado oil
1 tablespoon fresh lemon zest
1 tablespoon lemon juice
2 teaspoons honey

1 Make honey lemon dressing.

2 Segment oranges over small bowl; reserve juice.

3 Use vegetable peeler to cut cucumber into thin ribbons. Place cucumber in medium bowl with mint, orange segments, reserved juice and dressing; toss gently to combine. Season to taste.

honey lemon dressing Place ingredients in screw-top jar; shake well.

prep time 20 minutes **serves** 4

tip Traditionally served as an accompaniment to spicy dishes, this recipe would also make a great light vegetarian starter.

Valencian salad

6 large oranges, peeled, thinly sliced
2 tomatoes, thickly sliced
1 large red onion, thinly sliced
3 ounces manchego cheese, shaved
¾ cup pitted black olives, halved
2 large avocados, coarsely chopped
1 cup loosely packed fresh mint

orange dressing
2 tablespoons olive oil
2 tablespoons red wine vinegar
2 tablespoons orange juice
1 clove garlic, crushed

1 Make orange dressing.

2 Place orange in large bowl with remaining ingredients and dressing; toss gently to combine. Season to taste.

orange dressing Place ingredients in screw-top jar; shake well.

prep time 20 minutes **serves** 6

tip Manchego cheese is a sharp, firm Spanish cheese; it can be found in most specialty food stores and delicatessens. You can use Parmesan cheese instead, if manchego is not available.

Spinach, feta and pine nut salad

4 cups baby spinach leaves
1 cup each loosely packed fresh mint leaves and fresh dill leaves
2 ounces feta cheese, crumbled
½ cup pine nuts, toasted

lemon dressing
1 lemon
1 tablespoon olive oil
1 tablespoon oregano

1 Make lemon dressing.

2 Combine spinach, mint and dill in medium bowl.

3 Just before serving, add cheese, nuts and dressing; toss gently to combine.

lemon dressing Using a zester remove zest from lemon in long thin strips; place in small heatproof bowl. Add enough boiling water to cover zest; drain. Repeat process two more times. Remove remaining skin and pith from lemon. Segment flesh over small bowl to catch juice; coarsely chop flesh. Add well-drained zest and flesh to bowl with juice; add remaining ingredients, season to taste.

prep time 20 minutes **serves** 4

Beet salad

1 pound bunch baby beets
2 tablespoons olive oil
1 tablespoon red wine vinegar
1 tablespoon finely chopped fresh flat-leaf parsley
1 teaspoon finely chopped fresh dill
1 clove garlic, crushed

1 Discard leaves from beets; reserve stems. Wash beets and stems. Place beets in medium saucepan; cover with water. Bring to a boil; simmer, covered, about 30 minutes or until tender. Add stems 5 minutes before end of cooking time. Drain.

2 When beets are cool enough to handle, use disposable gloves to gently slip off skin from beets; discard skins. Slice beets and stems. Combine beets and stems in shallow bowl with combined remaining ingredients; season to taste.

prep + cook time 40 minutes (+ cooling) **serves** 4

tip Use disposable gloves when handling beets to prevent your hands becoming stained.

Tomato and herb salad

5　tomatoes, coarsely chopped
¼　cup coarsely chopped fresh flat-leaf parsley
2　tablespoons each coarsely chopped fresh mint and dill

dressing
2　cloves garlic, crushed
2　tablespoons lemon juice
1　tablespoon olive oil
2　teaspoons white wine vinegar

1 Make dressing.

2 Combine tomatoes, herbs and dressing in medium bowl.

dressing　Place ingredients in screw-top jar, season to taste; shake well.

prep time 15 minutes　**serves** 4

Eggplant salad

1 large eggplant (about 1 pound)

parsley dressing
¼ cup coarsely chopped fresh flat-leaf parsley
1 clove garlic, crushed
1 teaspoon oregano
2 tablespoons olive oil
1 tablespoon lemon juice

1 Preheat oven to 400°F (375°F convection).

2 Place eggplant on baking sheet; prick all over with a fork. Roast eggplant about 40 minutes, turning occasionally, until very soft. Cool; peel.

3 Meanwhile, make parsley dressing.

4 Tear eggplant flesh into long strips. Serve with dressing.

parsley dressing Combine ingredients in small bowl; season to taste.

prep + cook time 50 minutes (+ cooling) **serves** 4 as a side

Roasted eggplant with marjoram vinaigrette

 1 large eggplant (about 1 pound), sliced into ¼-inch rounds
 ¼ cup olive oil
 1 small red onion, thinly sliced
 ¼ cup sherry vinegar
 2 teaspoons sugar
 2 tablespoons finely chopped fresh marjoram
 ½ cup olive oil, extra

1 Preheat oven to 400°F (375°F convection).

2 Brush both sides of eggplant slices with oil; place, in single layer, on baking sheets lined with parchment paper. Roast about 25 minutes, turning eggplant slices once, until lightly browned both sides.

3 Meanwhile, combine onion, vinegar, sugar, marjoram and extra oil in small bowl; season to taste. Spoon onion mixture over eggplant.

4 Serve eggplant warm or at room temperature with crusty bread.

prep + cook time 50 minutes **serves** 6

Carrot, raisin and herb salad

2½ pounds baby carrots, trimmed
  1 teaspoon each ground cumin and sweet paprika
  ½ teaspoon ground cinnamon
  ¼ cup olive oil
  ¼ cup orange juice
  2 tablespoons lemon juice
  ⅓ cup raisins
  ⅔ cup coarsely chopped fresh flat-leaf parsley
  ¼ cup firmly packed fresh mint

1 Preheat oven to 400°F (375°F convection).

2 Combine carrots, spices and half the oil in large shallow baking dish; roast, uncovered, about 15 minutes or until carrots are tender. Cool 20 minutes.

3 Meanwhile, make dressing by combining juices, raisins, remaining oil and half the parsley in large bowl; season to taste.

4 Serve carrots drizzled with dressing; sprinkle with mint and remaining parsley.

prep + cook time 30 minutes (+ cooling) **serves** 6

tip You need 3 bunches of baby carrots to get 2½ pounds of trimmed carrots. If you're pressed for time, use pre-cleaned bags of baby carrots.

Radish and herb salad

2 large pita breads, cut into wedges
1 medium green bell pepper, finely chopped
1 cucumber, seeded, finely chopped
1 tomato, finely chopped
4 red radishes, coarsely grated
½ cup finely chopped fresh flat-leaf parsley
⅓ cup finely chopped fresh mint
¼ cup coarsely chopped fresh cilantro
2 tablespoons olive oil
2 tablespoons lemon juice
2 cloves garlic, crushed

1 Preheat broiler.

2 Place bread on baking sheets; toast under broiler about 5 minutes or until browned both sides and crisp.

3 Combine remaining ingredients in medium bowl; season to taste.

4 Serve salad with pita crisps.

prep + cook time 25 minutes **serves** 8

Artichokes in oregano vinaigrette

6 globe artichokes (about 2½ pounds)
½ cup lemon juice
⅓ cup olive oil
1 tablespoon white wine vinegar
2 cloves garlic, crushed
1 small red onion, thinly sliced
1 tablespoon fresh oregano

1 Prepare artichokes by snapping off tough outer leaves and peeling stems. Trim stems to 2 inches. Cut ¾ inch off top of artichokes to reveal chokes. Cut artichokes in quarters from top to bottom, then scoop out and discard furry chokes from centers. As you finish preparing each artichoke, place it in a large bowl of water containing half the juice (this stops any discoloration while you are preparing the next one).

2 Add artichoke and remaining juice to large pot of boiling water; boil, uncovered, about 20 minutes or until tender. Drain; cool.

3 Place artichokes in large bowl; pour over combined oil, vinegar and garlic. Cover; refrigerate 3 hours or overnight.

4 Combine artichoke mixture with onion; season to taste. Serve sprinkled with oregano.

prep + cook time 1 hour (+ refrigeration) **serves** 6

Zucchini with chermoulla dressing

2 tablespoons olive oil
2 tablespoons butter
8 zucchini, halved lengthways

chermoulla dressing
1 small red onion, finely chopped
2 cloves garlic, crushed
½ teaspoon hot paprika
1 teaspoon each sweet paprika and ground cumin
½ cup olive oil
2 tablespoons lemon juice
1 cup finely chopped fresh flat-leaf parsley

1 Heat oil and butter in large skillet; cook zucchini until browned lightly and tender.

2 Meanwhile, make chermoulla dressing.

3 Serve zucchini drizzled with dressing.

chermoulla dressing Place ingredients in screw-top jar; shake well.

prep + cook time 35 minutes **serves** 8

Green beans with tomato walnut sauce

2 pounds green beans, trimmed
1 can (15 ounces) crushed tomatoes
1 tablespoon olive oil
2 cloves garlic, crushed
2 teaspoons each ground coriander and cumin
¼ teaspoon cayenne pepper
¾ cup coarsely chopped toasted walnuts
½ cup coarsely chopped fresh cilantro
1 teaspoon white sugar
1 small red bell pepper, thinly sliced
1 small yellow bell pepper, thinly sliced

1 Boil, steam or microwave beans until tender; drain.

2 Blend or process undrained tomatoes until smooth.

3 Heat oil in large skillet; cook garlic, spices and nuts, stirring, until fragrant. Add tomatoes, fresh cilantro and sugar; cook, stirring, until heated through. Remove from heat, stir in bell peppers and beans, season to taste.

prep + cook time 25 minutes **serves** 6

Baked cabbage with tomatoes

1 can (14 ounces) crushed tomatoes
1 small onion, coarsely grated
1 clove garlic, crushed
1 teaspoon ground cumin
½ teaspoon white sugar
2 baby green cabbages, quartered
2 tablespoons olive oil
2 tablespoons coarsely chopped fresh flat-leaf parsley

1 Preheat oven to 325°F (300°F convection).

2 Combine undrained tomatoes, onion, garlic, cumin and sugar in small bowl; season to taste.

3 Place cabbage in medium ovenproof dish; top with tomato mixture. Bake, covered, about 30 minutes or until cabbage is tender.

4 Serve cabbage mixture drizzled with oil; sprinkle with parsley.

prep + cook time 40 minutes **serves** 6

tip If you can't find baby cabbage, use 1 small green cabbage and cut into eight wedges.

Spiced cauliflower couscous

1 tablespoon olive oil
1 onion, thinly sliced
1 teaspoon ground coriander
½ small cauliflower, cut into small florets
2 tablespoons water
⅓ cup coarsely chopped fresh cilantro
1¼ cups couscous
1¼ cups boiling water

1 Heat oil in large saucepan; cook onion, stirring, until soft. Add ground coriander and cauliflower; cook, stirring, until fragrant. Add the water; cook, covered, about 10 minutes or until cauliflower is tender and water is absorbed. Stir in half the fresh cilantro.

2 Meanwhile, combine couscous with the boiling water in large heatproof bowl, cover; stand about 5 minutes or until liquid is absorbed, fluffing with fork occasionally.

3 Stir cauliflower mixture into couscous; season to taste. Serve sprinkled with remaining fresh cilantro.

prep + cook time 25 minutes **serves** 6

Cauliflower with garlic, chilies and anchovies

4 pounds cauliflower, cut into small florets
⅓ cup extra virgin olive oil
2 fresh long red chilies, seeded, finely chopped
4 cloves garlic, finely chopped
6 drained anchovy fillets, finely chopped
1 cup coarsely chopped fresh flat-leaf parsley
2 tablespoons lemon juice
1 lemon, cut into wedges

1 Boil, steam or microwave cauliflower until almost tender; drain well.

2 Heat oil in large deep skillet; cook chilies, garlic and anchovies, stirring, until fragrant. Add cauliflower; cook, stirring, until hot. Remove from heat; stir in parsley and juice. Season to taste. Serve with lemon wedges.

prep + cook time 40 minutes **serves** 8

tip If you don't have a large skillet, toss the cauliflower with the anchovy mixture in a wok.

Spicy fried potatoes

2 pounds baby new potatoes
2 tablespoons olive oil
1 tablespoon harissa
2 cloves garlic, crushed
2 teaspoons cumin seeds
2 teaspoons fresh lemon zest
2 tablespoons finely chopped fresh flat-leaf parsley

1 Boil, steam or microwave potatoes until tender; drain, then cut in half.

2 Heat oil in large skillet; cook potatoes, harissa, garlic and seeds, stirring occasionally, about 10 minutes or until potatoes are browned. Stir in zest and parsley; season to taste.

prep + cook time 35 minutes **serves** 6

Slow-cooked potatoes with wine and herbs

1 lemon
1¼ pounds fingerling potatoes, halved lengthways
1 tablespoon olive oil
1 onion, thinly sliced
12 unpeeled garlic cloves
1 tablespoon dried oregano
4 bay leaves
½ cup dry white wine
1 cup chicken stock
⅓ cup kalamata olives
⅓ cup feta cheese, crumbled

1 Preheat oven to 325°F (300°F convection).

2 Finely grate zest from the lemon. Squeeze lemon; you need ¼ cup juice. Combine potatoes and juice in bowl; season.

3 Heat oil in large skillet; cook onion and garlic, stirring, until onion softens. Add potatoes with juice, oregano, zest and bay leaves; stir to coat in onion mixture. Add wine and stock; bring to the boil.

4 Transfer potato mixture to a medium baking dish. Roast, uncovered, stirring occasionally, about 40 minutes or until potatoes are tender.

5 Serve potatoes with olives and feta.

prep + cook time 55 minutes **serves** 4 as a side

Chorizo and potato tortilla

1½ pounds russet potatoes, thinly sliced
  1 tablespoon olive oil
  1 large onion, thinly sliced
  1 chorizo sausage (about 5 ounces), thinly sliced
  6 eggs, lightly beaten
  1 cup heavy cream
  4 scallions, thickly sliced
  ¼ cup coarsely grated mozzarella cheese
  ¼ cup coarsely grated Cheddar cheese

1 Boil, steam or microwave potato until tender; drain.

2 Meanwhile, heat oil in medium skillet; cook onion, stirring, until softened. Add chorizo; cook, stirring, until crisp. Drain chorizo mixture on paper towels.

3 Whisk eggs in large bowl with cream, scallions and cheeses, season; stir in potato and chorizo mixture.

4 Pour mixture into heated oiled medium skillet; cook, covered, over low heat, about 10 minutes or until tortilla is just set. Carefully invert tortilla onto plate, then slide back into pan; cook, uncovered, about 5 minutes or until cooked through.

prep + cook time 45 minutes **serves** 4

Honey-spiced carrots and sweet potatoes

 4 carrots
 2 small sweet potatoes, thickly sliced
 3 tablespoons butter, melted
 1 tablespoon olive oil
1½ teaspoons ground cumin
 1 teaspoon cumin seeds
 ¼ cup honey
 2 tablespoons coarsely chopped fresh flat-leaf parsley

1 Preheat oven to 425°F (400°F convection).

2 Cut carrots into 1½-inch pieces. Cook carrot and sweet potatoes in large saucepan of boiling water 5 minutes; drain.

3 Combine butter, oil, cumin, seeds and honey in small bowl. Place vegetables on oiled wire rack over large baking dish. Brush vegetables with honey-spice mixture. Roast, uncovered, about 20 minutes, brushing with remaining honey-spice mixture, until vegetables are tender.

4 Serve vegetables sprinkled with parsley.

prep + cook time 45 minutes **serves** 4

Spicy couscous

1 cup chicken stock
2 cups water
3 cups couscous
⅓ cup pine nuts, toasted
1 small red onion, finely chopped
½ cup dried currants
⅓ cup each coarsely chopped fresh mint and flat-leaf parsley

harissa dressing
2 teaspoons harissa
⅓ cup lemon juice
⅓ cup olive oil

1 Bring stock and water to a boil in medium saucepan.

2 Combine couscous and hot stock mixture in large heatproof bowl, cover; stand about 5 minutes or until liquid is absorbed, fluffing with fork occasionally.

3 Stir nuts, onion, currants and herbs into couscous.

4 Make harissa dressing.

5 Just before serving, pour dressing over couscous; toss gently.

harissa dressing Place ingredients in screw-top jar; shake well.

prep + cook time 15 minutes **serves** 8

Saffron cinnamon couscous

3½ cups chicken stock
1 teaspoon saffron threads
4 cinnamon sticks
3 cups couscous
2 tablespoons vegetable oil
2 red onions, finely chopped
3 cloves garlic, crushed
2 small fresh red Thai chilies, finely chopped
2 teaspoons ground cumin
¾ cup slivered almonds, roasted
1 cup coarsely chopped fresh cilantro

1 Bring stock, saffron and cinnamon to a boil in small saucepan. Reduce heat; simmer, covered, 15 minutes. Remove cinnamon.

2 Combine couscous and hot stock in large heatproof bowl, cover; stand about 5 minutes or until liquid is absorbed, fluffing with fork occasionally.

3 Meanwhile, heat oil in large frying pan; cook onion, garlic, chilies and cumin, stirring, until onion softens.

4 Add couscous to pan; stir until heated through. Stir in nuts and coriander; season to taste.

prep + cook time 20 minutes **serves** 8

tip This recipe is best made close to serving time.

Saffron rice with zucchini flowers

12 zucchini flowers, stem attached
 3 tablespoons butter
 1 large red onion, cut into wedges
 2 teaspoons caraway seeds
 1 clove garlic, crushed
 4 cups cooked white long-grain rice
 1 teaspoon ground turmeric
pinch saffron threads
 ¼ cup flaked almonds, toasted

1 Remove flowers from zucchini; discard stamens from flowers. Slice zucchini thinly.

2 Melt butter in large skillet; cook onion, seeds and garlic, stirring, until onion softens. Add sliced zucchini; cook, stirring, until tender. Add rice, spices and zucchini flowers; cook, stirring, until hot. Stir in half the nuts; season to taste.

3 Serve rice sprinkled with remaining nuts.

prep + cook time 30 minutes **serves** 4

tip The stem of zucchini is the baby zucchini attached to the flower. You need to cook about 1½ cups white long-grain rice for this recipe. Spread cooked rice on a flat tray and refrigerate, uncovered, overnight before using.

Olive and bell peppers brown rice

2 cups brown medium-grain rice
2 large red bell peppers
1 cup feta-stuffed green olives, thinly sliced
1 tablespoon finely chopped fresh oregano
1 fresh long red chili, finely chopped

red wine vinaigrette
2 tablespoons lemon juice
2 tablespoons red wine vinegar
2 tablespoons olive oil
½ teaspoon sugar
1 clove garlic, crushed

1 Cook rice in large saucepan of boiling water, uncovered, until tender; drain. Rinse under cold water; drain. Place in large bowl.

2 Meanwhile, quarter bell peppers; discard seeds and membranes. Cook bell peppers, skin-side up, under broiler until skin blisters and blackens. Transfer to a heatproof bowl. Cover bell peppers with paper or plastic for 5 minutes; peel away skin, then thinly slice.

3 Make red wine vinaigrette.

4 Add bell peppers, vinaigrette and remaining ingredients to rice; season to taste, mix gently.

red wine vinaigrette Place ingredients in screw-top jar; shake well.

prep + cook time 40 minutes **serves** 8

Seafood

Tuna souvlakia with roasted pepper salad

1¼ pounds tuna
2 tablespoons olive oil
1 tablespoon dried oregano
1 teaspoon red pepper flakes

roasted pepper salad
3 red bell peppers
3 yellow bell peppers
3 cloves garlic, thinly sliced
¾ cup loosely packed fresh oregano
2 tablespoons red wine vinegar

1 Cut tuna into 1¼-inch pieces. Combine tuna, oil, oregano and pepper flakes in medium bowl; season. Thread tuna onto eight metal skewers; place in shallow dish, cover, refrigerate 30 minutes.

2 Meanwhile, make roasted pepper salad.

3 Cook tuna in heated grill pan, until fish is opaque and cooked as desired.

4 Serve tuna with salad.

roasted pepper salad Cook bell peppers in heated grill pan over high heat, turning, until skin blackens. Place bell peppers in large bowl, cover with plastic wrap; cool. Peel away skin, then slice bell peppers thinly. Place bell peppers in medium bowl with garlic, oregano and vinegar; toss gently to combine. Season to taste.

prep + cook time 40 minutes (+ refrigeration & cooling) **serves** 4

Scallop and fish skewers with tomato salad

1 pound white fish fillets, cut into ¾-inch pieces
1 pound scallops
⅓ cup finely chopped fresh basil
¼ cup red wine vinegar
2 tablespoons olive oil
3 large roma tomatoes, cut into ½-inch pieces
½ pound yellow teardrop tomatoes, halved
½ pound cherry tomatoes, halved
½ cup loosely packed fresh basil leaves, torn

red wine vinaigrette
2 tablespoons red wine vinegar
¼ cup olive oil
1 teaspoon Dijon mustard
1 teaspoon sugar

1 Thread fish and scallops, alternately, onto 12 bamboo skewers; place in large shallow dish, drizzle with combined chopped basil, vinegar and oil.

2 Make red wine vinaigrette.

3 Cook skewers in heated oiled grill pan until fish is opaque and cooked through.

4 Meanwhile, combine tomatoes, torn basil and vinaigrette in medium bowl; season to taste.

5 Serve skewers with salad.

red wine vinaigrette Place ingredients in screw-top jar; shake well.

prep + cook time 40 minutes **serves** 4

tip Soak skewers in cold water before use to prevent them from splintering or scorching during cooking.

141

Herbed fish skewers with smashed potatoes and skordalia

1½ pounds white fish fillets, cut into ¾-inch pieces
¼ cup olive oil
2 tablespoons each finely chopped fresh flat-leaf parsley
and lemon thyme
2 pounds baby new potatoes, unpeeled
½ cup sour cream
3 tablespoons butter, softened

skordalia
1 small potato
1 slice white bread
2 cloves garlic, crushed
1 tablespoon cider vinegar
¼ cup water
2 tablespoons olive oil

1 Thread fish onto eight skewers; place in medium shallow dish. Brush with combined oil and herbs. Cover; refrigerate 20 minutes.

2 Meanwhile, make skordalia.

3 Boil, steam or microwave potatoes until tender; drain. Mash half the potatoes in medium bowl with sour cream and butter until smooth. Using fork, crush remaining potatoes until skins burst; fold into mash mixture. Cover to keep warm.

4 Cook skewers in heated oiled grill pan. Serve fish skewers with smashed potatoes and skordalia.

skordalia Boil, steam or microwave potato until tender; drain. Mash potato in medium bowl until smooth. Discard crusts from bread. Soak bread in small bowl of cold water; drain. Squeeze out excess liquid. Blend or process bread with remaining ingredients until smooth. Stir bread mixture into potato.

prep + cook time 50 minutes (+ refrigeration) **serves** 4

tip Soak bamboo skewers in water for 1 hour before using to prevent them from scorching during cooking.

Fish gyros

2 tablespoons olive oil
1 tablespoon red wine vinegar
2 tomatoes, cut into thin wedges
2 cups baby arugula
4 long thin white fish fillets (4 ounces each), halved
1 tablespoon finely chopped fresh oregano
4 8-inch flour tortillas
½ cup yogurt
1 clove garlic, crushed

1 Combine half the oil with vinegar, tomato and arugula in medium bowl.

2 Combine fish, oregano and remaining oil in medium bowl. Thread fish lengthways onto eight bamboo skewers. Cook skewers in heated oiled grill pan until cooked.

3 Wrap tortillas in foil; warm on heated grill plate about 2 minutes, turning once, or until heated through.

4 Serve warm tortillas topped with fish and salad; drizzle with combined yogurt and garlic.

prep + cook time 30 minutes **serves** 4

tip Soak bamboo skewers in cold water for at least an hour before using to prevent them from scorching during cooking.

Pan-fried fish with fennel and olive salad

4 white fish fillets (about 7 ounces each), skin-on
2 red bell peppers, coarsely chopped
2 small fennel, trimmed, thinly sliced
½ cup pitted black olives
⅓ cup coarsely chopped fresh basil
2 tablespoons olive oil
1 tablespoon balsamic vinegar

1 Cook fish, skin-side down, in heated oiled large skillet, turning once, until fish is opaque.

2 Meanwhile, place remaining ingredients in medium bowl, season to taste; toss gently to combine.

3 Serve fish with salad.

prep + cook time 20 minutes **serves** 4

Spiced fried fish with lemon pistachio couscous

  1 tablespoon all-purpose flour
1½ teaspoons each ground coriander and cumin
  1 teaspoon sweet smoked paprika
  ¼ teaspoon cayenne pepper
  8 white fish fillets (6 ounces each)
  1 tablespoon olive oil
  1 lemon cut into 8 wedges

lemon pistachio couscous

  1 cup couscous
  ¾ cup boiling water
  2 teaspoons fresh lemon zest
  ¼ cup lemon juice
  2 teaspoons olive oil
  1 small red onion, finely chopped
  1 clove garlic, crushed
  ½ cup roasted unsalted shelled pistachios
  ½ cup coarsely chopped fresh mint

1 Make lemon pistachio couscous.

2 Combine flour and spices in medium bowl; add fish, rub spice mixture all over fish.

3 Heat oil in large skillet; cook fish, in batches, until browned and cooked as desired.

4 Serve fish with couscous and wedges of lemon.

lemon pistachio couscous Combine couscous, the water, zest and juice in medium heatproof bowl, cover; stand about 5 minutes or until liquid is absorbed, fluffing with fork occasionally. Heat oil in small skillet; cook onion and garlic, stirring, until onion softens. Stir onion mixture, nuts and mint through couscous, season to taste.

prep + cook time 35 minutes **serves** 4

Lemon and herb fish with chickpea salad

 2 tablespoons olive oil
½ teaspoon red pepper flakes
 1 cup finely shredded fresh basil
 4 white fish fillets (about 7 ounces each), skin-on
 2 cloves garlic, thinly sliced
 2 cans (15 ounce) chickpeas, rinsed, drained
½ cup chicken stock
½ pound roasted red bell pepper in oil, drained, thickly sliced
 1 lemon

1 Combine half the oil with pepper flakes and a third of the basil in medium bowl. Cut two slits in skin of each fish fillet; add fish to oil mixture, turn to coat in mixture.

2 Cook fish, skin-side down, in large heated oiled skillet 2 minutes; turn, cook a further 3 minutes or until cooked through. Transfer to plate; cover, stand 5 minutes.

3 Heat remaining oil in same skillet; cook garlic, stirring, 30 seconds. Add chickpeas, stock and roasted pepper; simmer, uncovered, about 3 minutes or until stock is almost evaporated.

4 Meanwhile, using a vegetable peeler, peel zest from lemon; slice zest thinly. Juice lemon; add 2 tablespoons of juice to chickpeas with zest. Season to taste; stir in remaining basil.

5 Serve fish with chickpea salad.

prep + cook time 25 minutes **serves** 4

tip Look for roasted peppers in the salad bar or olive bar at your grocery store

Fish steaks with kalamata olive dressing

4   white fish steaks (about 7 ounces each)
2   teaspoons olive oil
1   cup coarsely chopped fresh flat-leaf parsley

kalamata olive dressing
1   red onion, thinly sliced
1   cup pitted kalamata olives, coarsely chopped
8   anchovies, drained, sliced thinly lengthways
1   tablespoon dried oregano
1   clove garlic, crushed
¼   cup red wine vinegar
¼   cup olive oil

1 Make kalamata olive dressing.

2 Brush steaks with oil; season. Cook steaks in heated grill pan until fish is opaque and cooked through.

3 Meanwhile, warm dressing in small saucepan; stir in parsley.

4 Serve steaks with dressing.

kalamata olive dressing Combine ingredients in medium bowl; season.

prep + cook time 20 minutes **serves** 4

tip Dressing can be made a day ahead, cover and refrigerate. We used swordfish in this recipe; tuna steaks and firm white fish cutlets would also be fine.

Crisp fish with paprika mustard butter

¼ cup olive oil
6 white fish fillets (about 7 ounces each), skin-on
1 small red onion, finely chopped
2 chorizo sausages (5 ounces each), coarsely chopped
½ pound cherry tomatoes, halved
1 can (15 ounces) cannellini beans, rinsed, drained
1 bag (5 ounces) baby spinach

paprika mustard butter
8 tablespoons (1 stick) butter, softened
2 teaspoons each Dijon and wholegrain mustard
½ teaspoon ground paprika
1 tablespoon fresh lemon zest
1 tablespoon finely chopped fresh flat-leaf parsley

1 Preheat oven to 400°F (375°F convection).

2 Make paprika mustard butter.

3 Heat 2 tablespoons of the oil in large skillet; cook fish, skin-side down, in batches, about 5 minutes or until skin is crisp. Transfer fish, skin-side up, to foil-lined baking sheet; roast, in oven, about 6 minutes or until fish is opaque and cooked through. Remove from oven, cover loosely with foil; stand 5 minutes.

4 Meanwhile, heat remaining oil in same cleaned skillet; cook onion, stirring, until softened. Add chorizo; cook, stirring, 1 minute. Stir in tomato and beans. Reduce heat; cook about 2 minutes or until beans are heated through. Stir in spinach; season to taste.

5 Divide bean mixture among serving plates, top with fish and a slice of paprika mustard butter.

paprika mustard butter Beat butter in small bowl with electric mixer until soft. Beat in remaining ingredients; season. Form mixture into log, roll in plastic wrap; refrigerate or freeze until firm.

prep + cook time 40 minutes (+ refrigeration) **serves** 6

Crisp-skinned fish with roast garlic skordalia

4 white fish fillets (about 7 ounces each), skin on

rosemary oil
- ¼ cup olive oil
- 4 cloves garlic, thinly sliced
- 2 tablespoons rosemary

roast garlic skordalia
- 2 bulbs garlic
- 1¼ pounds small potatoes
- ½ cup milk, warmed
- 1 tablespoon fresh lemon zest
- ½ cup olive oil
- ½ cup Greek-style yogurt
- ¼ cup lemon juice

1 Make rosemary oil and roast garlic skordalia.

2 Pat fish dry with paper towels; season. Heat 1 tablespoon of the rosemary oil in medium frying pan; cook fish, skin-side down, about 2 minutes or until skin is crisp. Turn fish, cook fish until opaque and cooked through.

3 Serve fish with skordalia, drizzled with rosemary oil.

rosemary oil Heat oil, garlic and rosemary in small saucepan over low heat until garlic begins to color. Cool.

roast garlic skordalia Preheat oven to 425°F (400°F convection). Wrap garlic in foil; place on oven tray with potatoes. Roast about 30 minutes or until garlic and potatoes are soft. Stand until cool enough to handle. Peel potatoes; place flesh in medium bowl. Squeeze garlic from cloves, add to potatoes with half the warm milk. Mash zest, garlic and potatoes until smooth. Gradually stir in oil, 1 tablespoon at a time. Stir in yogurt and juice; season to taste. Just before serving, heat remaining milk in medium saucepan; add skordalia, cook, stirring, until heated through.

prep + cook time 1 hour (+ cooling) **serves** 4

Salt-baked whole snapper with fennel and mint salad

3- pound whole snapper
1 large fennel bulb
1 lemon, thinly sliced
5 sprigs fresh thyme
6 pounds coarse cooking salt
8 egg whites

fennel and mint salad
2 zucchini
1 cup loosely packed fresh mint leaves
¼ cup olive oil
2 tablespoons red wine vinegar

1 Preheat oven to 425°F (400°F convection). Line large baking dish with parchment paper.

2 Clean fish, leave scales intact. Pat fish dry inside and out with paper towels. Season fish cavity. Remove stems from fennel. Fill fish cavity with lemon, thyme and fennel stems.

3 Combine salt and egg whites in large bowl. Spread half the mixture over base of dish, top with fish, then pack remaining salt mixture over fish to cover completely—the tail can be left out, if you like.

4 Bake fish about 35 minutes or until a skewer inserted into thickest part of fish feels hot when withdrawn. Stand fish 10 minutes before cracking the salt crust open.

5 Meanwhile, make fennel and mint salad.

6 Serve fish with salad.

fennel and mint salad Thinly shave fennel bulb lengthways; place in bowl of iced water. Using vegetable peeler, slice zucchini lengthways into ribbons. Combine zucchini and mint in bowl. Drain fennel, add to zucchini mixture with coarsely chopped fennel fronds, oil and vinegar; season to taste.

prep + cook time 1 hour **serves** 4

tip Use a mandolin or V-slicer to shave the fennel bulb for best results.

Baked fish with saffron, leek and potato

  2 tablespoons olive oil
1¼ pounds fingerling potatoes, thickly sliced
  2 leeks, thickly sliced
  4 cloves garlic, crushed
pinch saffron threads
  2 cups chicken stock
  4 (7 ounces each) white fish fillets

1 Preheat oven to 425°F (400°F convection).

2 Heat oil in large flameproof baking dish; cook potato, leek and garlic, stirring, until leek softens. Add saffron and stock; bring to a boil. Reduce heat; simmer, uncovered, 10 minutes.

3 Add fish, cover, transfer to oven; bake 20 minutes or until cooked through. Season to taste.

4 Serve fish topped with potato and leek; drizzle with pan juices.

prep + cook time 35 minutes **serves** 4

serving suggestion Sprinkle with fresh chervil leaves.

Fish parcels with anchovies and olives

4 white fish fillets (about 7 ounces each)
2 teaspoons fresh rosemary
4 drained anchovy fillets, finely chopped
2 teaspoons fresh lemon zest
2 cloves garlic, thinly sliced
½ cup pitted black olives
¼ cup coarsely chopped fresh flat-leaf parsley
1 tablespoon olive oil

1 Preheat oven to 425°F (400°F convection).

2 Divide fish among four 12-inch squares of baking paper. Top fish with combined remaining ingredients; season. Fold paper over fish, tucking ends under to secure.

3 Place parcels on oven tray; bake about 12 minutes or until fish is opaque and cooked through.

prep + cook time 25 minutes **serves** 4

serving suggestion Radicchio, arugula and tomato salad.

Oven-roasted fish with braised fennel

2 baby fennel bulbs
2 tablespoons olive oil
1 red onion, cut into thin wedges
1 cup large pitted green olives
1 lemon
1 cup dry white wine
½ cup fish stock
4 skinless white fish fillets (about 7 ounces each)

1 Preheat oven to 350°F (325°F convection).

2 Remove fennel fronds from tops of bulbs; coarsely chop, reserve. Slice fennel bulbs thickly lengthways.

3 Heat half the oil in large skillet over heat. Cook fennel, onion and olives, stirring, until lightly browned. Remove zest from lemon with zester, add to dish with wine and stock; bring to a boil. Transfer vegetables to medium baking dish; bake, uncovered, about 10 minutes or until fennel is soft. Season to taste.

4 Meanwhile, heat remaining oil in medium skillet. Pat fish dry; season. Brown fish lightly both sides—do not cook through.

5 Increase oven to 400°F (375°F convection). Place fish on top of fennel mixture; roast in oven about 5 minutes or until fish is cooked through. Serve sprinkled with reserved fennel fronds.

prep + cook time 35 minutes **serves** 4

Tuna with lentils and beans

    4 tuna steaks (6 ounces each)
    2 teaspoons each ground coriander and cumin
    ½ teaspoon red pepper flakes
    ¼ cup olive oil
    ⅓ cup finely chopped fresh flat-leaf parsley
    2 large carrots, cut into matchsticks
    2 cups chicken stock
    1 tablespoon honey
    1 cup brown lentils, rinsed, drained
    ¾ cup frozen fava beans, thawed, peeled
    1 tablespoon coarsely chopped fresh flat-leaf parsley, extra

1 Combine tuna, spices, chilli, half the oil and half the parsley in large bowl. Cover, refrigerate 3 hours or overnight.

2 Combine lentils with 1½ cups water in a medium saucepan. Bring to a boil; reduce heat and simmer 20-25 minutes until tender. Drain, if necessary.

3 Heat remaining oil in tagine or large skillet; cook carrots, stirring, until tender. Add stock, honey, lentils and half the beans; top with tuna. Bring to a boil, reduce heat; simmer, covered, about 10 minutes or until tuna is cooked as desired. Season to taste.

4 Stir in remaining beans; stand tagine, covered, 5 minutes. Serve sprinkled with extra parsley.

prep + cook time 50 minutes (+ refrigeration) **serves** 4

tip Ask your fish market to cut thick tuna steaks; thin steaks can easily overcook and dry out.

Roasted white fish with chermoulla

  4 whole baby snapper (about 12 ounces each)
  1 teaspoon ground cumin
 ½ teaspoon hot paprika
  2 teaspoons fresh lemon zest
  1 tablespoon olive oil

chermoulla

 ¼ cup olive oil
 ⅓ cup each finely chopped fresh flat-leaf parsley and coriander (cilantro)
  2 tablespoons lemon juice
  1 clove garlic, crushed
  1 fresh long red chili, finely chopped

1 Preheat oven to 400°F (375°F convection). Coat baking sheet with olive oil.

2 Score fish through thickest part of flesh. Rub fish all over with combined spices, zest and oil; season. Place fish on sheet; roast, uncovered, about 25 minutes or until cooked through.

3 Meanwhile, make chermoulla.

4 Serve fish drizzled with chermoulla; accompany with steamed couscous and a green salad, if desired.

chermoulla Combine ingredients in small bowl; season to taste.

prep + cook time 35 minutes **serves** 4

Grilled seafood with aïoli

1   pound uncooked large shrimp
½   cup olive oil
1   clove garlic, crushed
1   teaspoon sweet paprika
2   teaspoons fresh lemon zest
1¼ pounds white fish fillets
2   large zucchini, sliced thickly lengthways
1   large red bell pepper, quartered
1   lemon, cut into wedges

aïoli
½   cup mayonnaise
1   clove garlic, crushed
1   tablespoon lemon juice

1 Make aïoli.

2 Shell and devein shrimp, leaving tails intact. Place shrimp in large bowl with oil, garlic, paprika, zest and fish; toss to combine, season.

3 Cook vegetables in heated oiled grill pan until tender. Remove from heat; cover to keep warm.

4 Cook seafood in same heated grill pan until shrimp are changed in color and fish is opaque and cooked through.

5 Serve seafood and vegetables with aïoli and lemon wedges.

aïoli Combine ingredients in small bowl.

prep + cook time 35 minutes **serves** 4

Grilled salmon with chermoulla sauce

6 salmon fillets (6-ounces each), skin on
2 tablespoons olive oil
2 red onions
3 zucchini, thinly sliced lengthways
¾ pound asparagus, trimmed

chermoulla sauce
½ cup each firmly packed fresh flat-leaf parsley and cilantro
2 cloves garlic, coarsely chopped
1 teaspoon each red pepper flakes, ground coriander and cumin
½ teaspoon ground turmeric
1 tablespoon lemon juice
1 tablespoon olive oil
½ cup Greek-style yogurt

1 Make chermoulla sauce.

2 Rub fish skin with a little of the oil.

3 Cut each onion into 8 wedges, keeping root ends intact. Combine onion, zucchini and asparagus with remaining oil in medium bowl.

4 Cook fish in heated grill pan, skin-side down, until crisp; turn, cook as desired. Cook vegetables in another grill pan or lightly oiled skillet at the same time as the fish until tender.

5 Serve fish and vegetables with sauce; accompany with couscous, if desired.

chermoulla sauce Blend or process herbs, garlic, red pepper and ground spices until combined. Add juice and oil; process until smooth. Transfer to medium bowl; stir in yogurt, season to taste.

prep + cook time 30 minutes **serves** 6

tip Prepare the vegetables and the sauce up to a day ahead; keep the sauce, covered, in the refrigerator.

Grilled salmon with pepper and olive salsa

3 pound side of salmon, skin-on
2 teaspoons kosher salt
½ cup loosely packed fresh basil

olive salsa
1 large red bell pepper
½ pint cherry tomatoes, halved
2 tablespoons rinsed, drained baby capers
¼ cup pitted green olives, quartered
¼ cup olive oil

1 Make olive salsa.

2 Place double layer of foil about 3 feet long on flat work surface; coat with cooking oil spray. Place an 18-inch sheet of parchment paper in center of foil.

3 Pat salmon dry with paper towels; rub salt over skin. Place salmon, skin-side-down, onto baking paper. Fold foil and baking paper to enclose salmon securely.

4 Cook salmon parcel, skin-side-down, in heated oiled grill pan, over medium heat, about 10 minutes or until opaque and cooked to your liking.

5 Just before serving, stir basil into salsa; serve salmon topped with salsa.

olive salsa Preheat broiler. Quarter bell pepper; discard seeds and membranes. Cook bell pepper, skin-side-up, under grill until skin blisters and blackens. Cover bell pepper with paper or plastic wrap; stand 5 minutes. Peel away skins; cut into ¾-inch pieces. Place bell pepper in medium bowl with tomato, capers, olives and oil; toss gently to combine.

prep + cook time 40 minutes **serves** 8

tip The salmon can be prepared and wrapped up to one hour ahead. The salsa can be made two hours ahead; add basil just before serving.

Fish tagine

4 white fish fillets (about 7 pounds), skin on
1 tablespoon fresh lemon zest
2 teaspoons red pepper flakes
2 cloves garlic, crushed
1 tablespoon mustard seed oil
2 tablespoons butter
2 baby fennel bulbs, trimmed, cut into wedges
¼ pound green beans, halved lengthways
⅓ cup raisins
1 cup dry white wine
pinch saffron threads
⅓ cup roasted unsalted shelled pistachios

1 Combine fish, rind, pepper flakes, garlic and oil in large bowl. Cover; refrigerate 3 hours or overnight.

2 Melt butter in tagine or large skillet; cook fennel, stirring, until browned lightly. Add beans, raisins, wine and saffron; top with fish. Bring to a boil. Reduce heat; simmer, covered, about 15 minutes or until fish is cooked as desired. Season to taste.

3 Serve tagine sprinkled with nuts.

prep + cook time 30 minutes (+ refrigeration) **serves** 4

tip Fish or chicken stock can be used instead of wine. Mustard seed oil is available from health-food shops, delicatessens and some supermarkets. If you like, use olive oil instead.

Salt cod and potato pie

You will need to start this recipe 24 hours ahead.

  3 pounds salt cod
  2 tablespoons olive oil
  2 onions, thinly sliced
  4 cloves garlic, crushed
1½ cups white long-grain rice
  1 cup coarsely chopped fresh flat-leaf parsley
  ½ cup coarsely chopped fresh dill
  8 small potatoes, thinly sliced
  6 cups fish stock
  2 tablespoons coarsely chopped flat-leaf parsley, extra

1 Soak cod in cold water for 8 hours, changing the water twice.

2 Heat oil in large skillet; cook onion and garlic, stirring, until onion softens. Transfer to bowl; stir in rice and herbs. Season with pepper.

3 Preheat oven to 400°F (375°F convection). Drain cod. Remove skin, cut cod into large pieces, discarding any bones; gently stir into rice mixture.

4 Cover base of deep 16-cup ovenproof dish with one-third of the potato. Top with half the fish mixture; repeat layers with remaining potato and fish mixture, ending with potato. Place dish on oven tray, pour stock into dish.

5 Bake pie, uncovered, about 1¾ hours or until potatoes are tender. Stand 10 minutes. Sprinkle with extra parsley before serving.

prep + cook time 2 hours 30 minutes (+ standing) **serves** 8

tip Salt cod is available from most gourmet grocery stores.

Shrimp and zucchini with mint pilaf

20 uncooked large shrimp
4 tablespoons butter
1 tablespoon olive oil
1 white onion, finely chopped
2 cloves garlic, finely chopped
1 fresh small red chili, finely chopped
1½ cups white long-grain rice
1 teaspoon fresh lemon zest
¼ cup dry white wine
1½ cups hot fish stock
3 zucchini, coarsely grated

minted lemon dressing
2 lemons, peeled, segmented
1 cup loosely packed fresh flat-leaf parsley
½ cup loosely packed fresh mint
¼ cup olive oil

1 Shell and devein shrimp, leaving tails intact; refrigerate.

2 Heat butter and oil in medium heavy-based saucepan; cook onion, garlic and chilies, stirring, until onion softens. Add rice, zest and wine; cook until liquid has evaporated. Stir in hot stock, bring to a boil. Reduce heat to low, stirring; cook, covered, 10 minutes.

3 Meanwhile, make mint dressing.

4 Stir zucchini into rice mixture; top with shrimp. Cover; cook 5 minutes. Remove from heat; stand, covered, 5 minutes.

5 Serve pilaf drizzled with dressing.

minted lemon dressing Process ingredients until finely chopped. Season to taste.

prep + cook time 40 minutes **serves** 4

Shrimp and couscous salad with lemon cilantro dressing

1 cup couscous
1 cup boiling water
1 pound cooked shrimp
1 cucumber, thinly sliced
1 red bell pepper, finely chopped
1 cup loosely packed fresh cilantro
1 cup firmly packed trimmed watercress

lemon cilantro dressing
1 teaspoon fresh lemon zest
⅓ cup lemon juice
2 cloves garlic, crushed
¼ cup fish sauce
¼ cup coarsely chopped fresh cilantro

1 Make lemon cilantro dressing.

2 Combine couscous and the water in large heatproof bowl, cover; stand about 5 minutes or until liquid is absorbed, fluffing with fork occasionally.

3 Meanwhile, shell and devein shrimp, leaving tails intact.

4 Stir shrimp, dressing and remaining ingredients into couscous.

lemon cilantro dressing Place ingredients in screw-top jar, season to taste; shake well.

prep time 25 minutes **serves** 4

Shrimp souvlakia with tomato and fennel sauce

16 uncooked large shrimp
2 tablespoons olive oil
3 cloves garlic, crushed
2 teaspoons dried mint
1 teaspoon fresh lemon zest
2 tablespoons lemon juice

tomato and fennel sauce
2 baby fennel
1 tablespoon olive oil
1 onion, finely chopped
2 cloves garlic, finely chopped
3 ripe tomatoes, coarsely chopped
¼ cup ouzo or pernod
1 cup coarsely chopped fresh mint

1 Shell and devein shrimp, leaving tails intact. Combine shrimp in large bowl with remaining ingredients. Cover; refrigerate 1 hour.

2 Make tomato and fennel sauce.

3 Thread shrimp onto eight metal skewers; reserve marinade. Cook shrimp in heated oiled grill pan, until shrimp change color and are cooked through.

4 Serve shrimp with sauce.

tomato and fennel sauce Separate and finely chop fennel and fronds; reserve fennel fronds. Heat oil in medium saucepan over medium heat; cook onion, garlic and fennel until softened. Add tomato and ouzo; cook until heated through. Just before serving, stir in fronds and mint; season to taste.

prep + cook time 35 minutes (+ refrigeration) **makes** 8
serving suggestion Rice pilaf.

Chermoulla shrimp skewers

16 uncooked large shrimp
 1 tablespoon olive oil
 2 tablespoons each finely chopped fresh flat-leaf parsley, cilantro and mint
 2 cloves garlic, crushed
 2 teaspoons fresh lemon zest
 1 tablespoon lemon juice
 1 teaspon each ground allspice and caraway seeds

1 Shell and devein shrimp, leaving tails intact. Combine shrimp with oil, herbs, garlic, zest, juice, and spices in medium bowl; season.

2 Preheat broiler.

3 Thread shrimp, tail-end first, onto 16 bamboo skewers; cook shrimp under grill about 5 minutes or until changed in color.

prep + cook time 30 minutes **makes** 16

tip Soak bamboo skewers in cold water for at least an hour before using to prevent them burning during cooking.

Garlic shrimp

1¼ cups olive oil
¾ cup dry white wine
2 tablespoons lemon juice
6 cloves garlic, thinly sliced
1 fresh long red chili, finely chopped
2 pounds uncooked large shrimp
⅓ cup coarsely chopped fresh flat-leaf parsley

1 Preheat oven to 425°F (400°F convection).

2 Stir oil, wine, juice, garlic and chili in large flameproof baking dish over low heat 5 minutes or until fragrant. Cool 15 minutes.

3 Meanwhile, shell and devein shrimp, leaving tails intact.

4 Add shrimp to oil mixture; mix well. Transfer to oven; bake 10 minutes or until shrimp change color. Season to taste.

5 Spoon shrimp mixture in shallow bowls; sprinkle with parsley.

prep + cook time 45 minutes (+ cooling) **serves** 4

serving suggestion Crusty bread to soak up the juices.

Soft shell crabs with green onion aïoli

½ cup rice flour
1 teaspoon red pepper flakes
2 teaspoons salt
8 uncooked small soft shell crabs (about 1 pound)
vegetable oil, for deep-frying
1 cup loosely packed fresh basil leaves

green onion aïoli
¾ cup mayonnaise
2 scallions, thinly sliced
1 clove garlic, crushed
1 tablespoon lemon juice

1 Make green onion aïoli.

2 Combine flour, pepper flakes and salt in medium bowl.

3 Clean crabs; pat dry, then cut into quarters. Coat crabs with flour mixture; shake off excess.

4 Heat oil in large saucepan; deep-fry basil about 30 seconds or until crisp. Drain on paper towels. Deep-fry crabs, in batches, until lightly browned. Drain on paper towels.

5 Serve crabs with basil, aïoli and lemon wedges, if desired.

green onion aïoli Combine ingredients in small bowl.

prep + cook time 30 minutes **serves** 8

tip To clean the soft shell crabs, lift back the flap on undersides and wipe clean with a damp piece of paper towel. Never wash seafood under a running tap as this will wash away the "sea" flavor and waterlog the seafood. If you need to rinse, hold the seafood in one hand over the sink and use your other hand to gently splash the seafood with as little water as possible.

Mussels with tomato and chili

1 tablespoon olive oil
4 pounds black mussels
4 shallots, thinly sliced
4 cloves garlic, thinly sliced
3 fresh long red chilies, thinly sliced lengthways
1 cup dry white wine
1 pint cherry tomatoes
½ cup coarsely chopped fresh flat-leaf parsley

1 Heat oil in large saucepan; cook tomatoes until they begin to soften. Add shallot, garlic and chilies and cook, stirring, until fragrant.

2 Stir in wine; bring to a boil. Add mussels; cook, covered, about 3 minutes or until mussels open (discard any that do not). Season to taste; stir in parsley.

prep + cook time 25 minutes **serves** 4

tip Before you begin, make sure mussels have been scrubbed and bearded and are ready to cook.

Clams with white wine and tomatoes

5 pounds clams
½ cup dry white wine
½ cup olive oil
1 small red onion, finely chopped
2 cloves garlic, crushed
2 tablespoons lemon juice
2 tablespoons white wine vinegar
5 large tomatoes, coarsely chopped
4 scallions, thinly sliced
2 tablespoons coarsely chopped fresh cilantro

1 Rinse clams under cold water; place in large bowl of cold salted water, stand 2 hours. Discard water then rinse clams thoroughly; drain.

2 Place clams in large saucepan with wine. Cover; bring to a boil. Reduce heat; simmer about 5 minutes or until clams open (discard any that do not). Drain clams; discard liquid.

3 Heat one tablespoon of the oil in same pan; cook red onion and garlic, stirring, until lightly browned. Add combined juice, vinegar and remaining oil; cook, stirring, about 2 minutes or until slightly thickened.

4 Return clams to pan with tomato, green onion and cilantro; toss gently to combine. Season to taste.

prep + cook time 40 minutes (+ standing) **serves** 4

Poultry

Chicken with lentil salsa

12 chicken tenderloins
 2 teaspoons each ground cumin and ground coriander
 1 teaspoon ground turmeric
1½ cups red lentils
 1 clove garlic, crushed
 1 fresh small red Thai chili, finely chopped
 1 cucumber, seeded, finely chopped
 1 red bell pepper, finely chopped
¼ cup lemon juice
 2 teaspoons peanut oil
 2 tablespoons coarsely chopped fresh cilantro
 2 limes, cut into wedges

1 Combine chicken and spices in medium bowl.

2 Cook lentils in large saucepan of boiling water, uncovered, until tender; drain. Rinse under cold water; drain.

3 Place lentils in large bowl with garlic, chili, cucumber, bell pepper, juice, oil and fresh cilantro; toss gently to combine. Season to taste.

4 Cook chicken in heated oiled grill pan until cooked through. Cook limes in same grill pan until browned both sides.

5 Serve chicken with lentil salsa and lime wedges.

prep + cook time 25 minutes **serves** 4

Grilled chicken with tomato salad

2   tablespoons lemon juice
1   tablespoon sumac
2   teaspoons finely chopped fresh oregano
2   tablespoons olive oil
6   boneless, skinless chicken breasts, (about 6 ounces each)
3   lemons, halved
3   large pita bread

tomato salad
2   tablespoons lemon juice
2   tablespoons olive oil
1   pound grape tomatoes, halved
2   cucumbers, cut into ribbons
1   cup each firmly packed fresh flat-leaf parsley and fresh mint
2   teaspoons finely chopped fresh oregano
8   scallions, thinly sliced

1 Combine juice, sumac, oregano and half the oil in large bowl with chicken. Cover; refrigerate 3 hours or overnight.

2 Make minted tomato salad.

3 Cook chicken in grill pan until browned both sides and cooked through. Stand 5 minutes, then slice thickly.

4 Cook lemon, cut-side down, about 3 minutes or until lightly browned. Brush bread, both sides, with remaining oil; lightly brown in grill pan, break into coarse pieces.

5 Combine salad and bread; serve with chicken and lemon.

tomato salad Whisk juice and oil in large serving bowl, add remaining ingredients; toss gently to combine.

prep + cook time 35 minutes (+ refrigeration) **serves** 6

tip Refrigerate the chicken overnight, if you can, for the best flavor. Salad ingredients can be prepared ahead; assemble just before serving.

Grilled chicken with green olive butter

¾ pound baby new potatoes, thickly sliced
4 boneless, skinless chicken breasts (about 6 ounces each)
4 cups baby spinach

green olive butter

6 tablespoons butter, softened
¾ cup pitted green olives, coarsely chopped
1 teaspoon fresh lemon zest
1 clove garlic, crushed
1 tablespoon coarsely chopped fresh basil

1 Make green olive butter.

2 Boil, steam or microwave potato until tender; drain. Cover to keep warm.

3 Meanwhile, halve chicken fillets horizontally. Cook chicken in heated oiled grill pan until cooked through.

4 Divide potato among plates; top with spinach, chicken, then olive butter.

green olive butter Combine ingredients in small bowl.

prep + cook time 35 minutes **serves** 4

Chicken and chorizo salad with garlic mayonnaise

- 1 chorizo sausage (5 ounces), thinly sliced
- 4 boneless, skinless chicken breasts (about 6 ounces each)
- ¾ cup pimiento-stuffed green olives
- 3 pieces bottled roasted red bell pepper, drained, thinly sliced
- ½ small red onion, thinly sliced
- 2 cups loosely packed fresh flat-leaf parsley leaves
- ⅓ cup toasted almonds
- 1 lemon, cut into wedges

garlic mayonnaise
- ½ cup mayonnaise
- 1 clove garlic, crushed
- ½ teaspoon smoked paprika
- 1 tablespoon lemon juice

1 Make garlic mayonnaise.

2 Cook chorizo in heated medium skillet until browned and crisp; drain on paper towels.

3 Cook chicken in same pan until browned and cooked through. Remove from pan; cover, stand 5 minutes, then slice thinly.

4 Meanwhile, combine olives, roasted pepper, onion, parsley, nuts and chorizo in large bowl; season to taste.

5 Divide salad among serving plates; top with sliced chicken and garlic mayonnaise. Serve with lemon wedges.

garlic mayonnaise Combine ingredients in small bowl.

prep + cook time 40 minutes **serves** 4

tip The garlic mayonnaise can be thinned with a little boiling water, if you prefer.

Chicken with almond sauce

¼ cup olive oil
½ cup orange juice
3 cloves garlic, crushed
6 boneless, skinless chicken breasts (about 6 ounces each)
3 small fennel bulbs
2 red onions
1 tablespoon olive oil, extra

almond sauce
1 tablespoon olive oil
¼ cup stale breadcrumbs
¾ cup ground almonds
pinch ground cloves
1 cup chicken stock
2 tablespoons dry white wine
¼ cup heavy cream

1 Combine oil, juice, garlic and chicken in medium bowl. Cook chicken in heated oiled grill pan until browned and cooked through. Remove from heat; cover to keep warm.

2 Meanwhile, cut fennel and onions into wedges. Heat extra oil in large skillet; cook fennel and onion, stirring, until onions are soft and lightly browned. Remove from heat; cover to keep warm.

3 Make almond sauce.

4 Serve chicken with fennel mixture and sauce.

almond sauce Heat oil in medium skillet; cook breadcrumbs, stirring, until lightly browned. Add ground almonds and clove; cook, stirring, until lightly browned. Gradually add combined stock and wine, stir over heat until mixture is smooth; bring to a boil. Remove from heat; stir in cream. Season to taste.

prep + cook time 35 minutes **serves** 6

Chermoulla chicken with onion couscous

4 boneless skinless chicken breast fillets (6 ounces each)
2 tablespoons harissa

chermoulla
¾ cup lemon juice
¼ teaspoon saffron threads
1 teaspoon each ground cumin and red pepper flakes
½ teaspoon each smoked paprika and ground cinnamon
1 small onion, finely chopped
¾ cup coarsely chopped fresh cilantro
⅔ cup olive oil

onion couscous
1½ cups chicken stock
1½ cups couscous
1 tablespoon olive oil
1 large onion, thinly sliced
4 wedges preserved lemon
1 can (15 ounces) chickpeas, rinsed, drained
¼ teaspoon each ground allspice and cinnamon

1 Make chermoulla; reserve ⅓ cup chermoulla for serving.

2 Split each chicken breast in half horizontally to form 8 thin pieces. Combine chicken and remaining chermoulla in medium bowl, cover; refrigerate 3 hours or overnight.

3 Make onion couscous.

4 Drain chicken; cook in heated oiled grill pan until browned and cooked.

5 Serve chicken and couscous with reserved chermoulla and harissa.

chermoulla Stand juice and saffron in bowl 10 minutes. Toast spices in small skillet until fragrant. Combine spices, saffron mixture and remaining ingredients in medium bowl, season to taste.

onion couscous Bring stock to a boil in small saucepan. Combine couscous and hot stock in medium heatproof bowl, cover; stand 5 minutes or until liquid is absorbed, fluffing with fork occasionally. Heat oil in medium skillet; cook onion, stirring, until soft. Remove flesh from preserved lemon and discard; chop zest finely. Stir onion, preserved lemon, chickpeas and spices into couscous; cover to keep warm.

prep + cook time 55 minutes (+ refrigeration) **serves** 4

Chicken with olives and couscous

1 tablespoon olive oil
4 boneless skinless chicken breast (about 6 ounces each)
1 onion, thinly sliced
1 clove garlic, crushed
2 teaspoons ground cumin
¾ teaspoon ground turmeric
2 cinnamon sticks
3 (2¼-inch) strips lemon zest
1 tablespoon lemon juice
2 cups chicken stock
2 teaspoons cornstarch
1 tablespoon water
¾ cup pitted green olives
1 cup couscous
1 cup boiling water
½ cup coarsely chopped fresh cilantro

1 Heat oil in large skillet; cook chicken until browned both sides. Remove from skillet.

2 Cook onion, garlic and spices in same skillet, stirring, until onion softens. Return chicken to pan with rind, juice and stock; bring to a boil. Reduce heat; simmer, covered, about 15 minutes or until chicken is tender. Add blended cornstarch and the water; cook, stirring, until mixture boils and thickens. Discard zest and cinnamon sticks; stir in olives, season to taste.

3 Meanwhile, combine couscous and the boiling water in large heatproof bowl. Cover; stand about 5 minutes or until liquid is absorbed, fluffing with fork occasionally.

4 Serve chicken mixture with couscous, sprinkled with coriander.

prep + cook time 40 minutes **serves** 4

Spicy chicken and rice

      2 teaspoons olive oil
      1 large onion, coarsely chopped
      2 cloves garlic, crushed
      2 medium green bell peppers, coarsely chopped
     16 chicken drumettes (about 4 pounds)
      1 can (14 ounces) crushed tomato
      1 teaspoon hot paprika
      1 tablespoon each ground coriander and ground cumin
     ½ teaspoon cayenne pepper
      2 cups fresh corn kernels
     ½ cup dry red wine
      1 cup chicken stock
      2 dried bay leaves
    1½ cups white long-grain rice
      2 tablespoons finely chopped fresh flat-leaf parsley

1 Preheat oven to 400°F (375°F convection).

2 Heat oil in large flameproof casserole dish; cook onion, garlic and bell peppers, stirring, until vegetables soften. Remove vegetables, leaving as much oil in dish as possible.

3 Cook chicken in same dish, in batches, until browned. Remove from dish.

4 Return chicken and vegetables to dish with crushed tomatoes, spices, corn, wine, stock, bay leaves and rice; bring to a boil. Cover; bake in oven about 30 minutes or until rice is tender and chicken is cooked through. Season to taste. Serve sprinkled with parsley.

prep + cook time 1 hour **serves** 8

tip Chicken drumettes is the small fleshy part of the wing between shoulder and elbow, trimmed to resemble a drumstick.

serving suggestion Steamed green beans and crunchy bread rolls.

Chicken kebabs with harissa mayonnaise

2 tablespoons pistachio dukkah
1½ teaspoons mild paprika
2 tablespoons olive oil
6 boneless skinless chicken thighs, halved lengthways
1 lemon, cut into wedges

harissa mayonnaise
½ cup mayonnaise
2 teaspoons harissa
2 teaspoons lemon juice

1 Combine dukkah, paprika and oil in medium bowl, season; add chicken, turn to coat in mixture. Thread chicken onto twelve bamboo skewers.

2 Cook kebabs in heated oiled grill pan until chicken is cooked through.

3 Meanwhile, make harissa mayonnaise.

4 Serve kebabs with harissa mayonnaise and lemon wedges.

harissa mayonnaise Combine ingredients in small bowl.

prep + cook time 25 minutes **serves** 4

tip Dukkah is a Middle Eastern seed, nut and spice mix. Soak bamboo skewers in cold water for at least an hour before using to prevent them from burning during cooking.

214

Grilled chicken with Spanish rice

⅓ cup lemon juice
1 tablespoon olive oil
1 tablespoon sweet paprika
2 teaspoons dried oregano
2 fresh small red Thai chilies, finely chopped
1 clove garlic, crushed
4 boneless, skinless chicken thighs (about 6 ounces each), halved
⅓ cup tomato chutney or salsa

spanish rice
1 tablespoon olive oil
4 scallions, finely chopped
1 clove garlic, crushed
1 red bell pepper, finely chopped
1 cup canned corn kernels, rinsed, drained
3 cups cooked white long-grain rice
⅓ cup pitted green olives, coarsely chopped
¼ cup finely chopped fresh cilantro

1 Combine juice, oil, paprika, oregano, chilies, garlic and chicken in large bowl; season. Cook chicken mixture in heated oiled grill pan, covered loosely with foil, until browned both sides and cooked through.

2 Meanwhile, make Spanish rice.

3 Serve chicken with Spanish rice and tomato chutney or salsa.

Spanish rice Heat oil in large skillet; cook onion, garlic, bell pepper and corn, stirring, until vegetables soften. Add rice; cook, stirring, about 5 minutes or until heated through. Stir in olives and cilantro; season to taste.

prep + cook time 35 minutes **serves** 4

tip For a more intense flavor, marinate the chicken overnight.

You will need to cook 1 cup white long-grain rice for the amount of cooked rice needed for this recipe.

217

Chicken tagine with dried plums

   4 whole chicken legs (about 3 pounds)
   2 tablespoons Moroccan seasoning
   ¼ cup all-purpose flour
   1 tablespoon olive oil
   8 shallots
   1 cup pitted dried plums, halved
   ¾ cup blanched almonds, toasted
   ½ pound Swiss chard leaves, finely shredded
   2 cups chicken stock
   ½ cup prune juice
   2 tablespoons finely chopped fresh flat-leaf parsley

1 Preheat oven to 400°F (375°F convection).

2 Rinse chicken under cold water; pat dry inside and out with paper towels.

3 Combine seasoning and flour in large bowl; coat chicken with flour mixture, shake off excess.

4 Heat oil in tagine or flameproof casserole dish on stove top; cook chicken, in batches, until browned. Remove from tagine; drain on paper towels.

5 Meanwhile, peel shallots, leaving root ends intact. Cook shallots in same heated tagine, stirring, until browned. Add plums, nuts, half the Swiss chard, stock, juice and parsley; bring to a boil. Top with chicken.

6 Cover tagine, transfer to oven; bake about 50 minutes or until chicken is cooked. Remove from oven; stir in remaining Swiss chard. Season to taste. Let stand tagine, covered, 10 minutes before serving.

prep + cook time 1 hour 5 minutes **serves** 4

tip Use either canned or packaged stock for a good flavor.

Chicken tagine with figs and walnuts

½ cup coarsely chopped walnuts
4 chicken drumsticks
4 boneless chicken thigh
2 teaspoons cumin seeds
2 teaspoons each ground ginger and cinnamon
1 tablespoon olive oil
1 large red onion, thickly sliced
pinch saffron threads

1½ cups chicken stock
1 tablespoon honey
6 medium fresh figs, halved
1 teaspoon sugar
2 cups baby spinach
¼ cup finely chopped fresh flat-leaf parsley

1 Toast nuts in dry skillet until fragrant.

2 Combine chicken and cumin seeds with half the ginger and half the cinnamon in large bowl.

3 Heat oil in tagine or large flameproof casserole dish; cook chicken, in batches, until browned. Remove from tagine. Reserve 1 tablespoon pan juices; discard remainder.

4 Heat reserved pan juices in same tagine; cook onion, stirring, until soft. Add saffron and remaining ginger and cinnamon; cook, stirring, about 2 minutes or until fragrant. Return chicken to tagine with stock; bring to a boil. Reduce heat; simmer, covered, about 30 minutes or until chicken is cooked.

5 Remove chicken from tagine; cover to keep warm. Add honey to tagine; simmer, uncovered, about 10 minutes or until sauce is browned and slightly thickened.

6 Meanwhile, preheat broiler. Place figs, cut-side up, on a baking sheet lined with parchment paper; sprinkle with sugar. Broil about 5 minutes or until lightly browned.

7 Return chicken to tagine with spinach; simmer, covered, until heated through. Season to taste.

8 Serve tagine topped with figs; sprinkle with nuts and parsley.

prep + cook time 1 hour 10 minutes **serves** 6

Braised chicken with chickpeas, lemon and garlic

1   tablespoon olive oil
2   onions, thickly sliced
2   teaspoons smoked paprika
3   cloves garlic, crushed
8   boneless, skinless chicken thighs (about 3 pounds)
3   cups chicken stock
¼   cup lemon juice
2   fresh long red chilies, halved lengthways
2   cans (15 ounces) chickpeas, rinsed, drained
2   teaspoons Dijon mustard
½   cup coarsely chopped fresh flat-leaf parsley
2   teaspoons fresh lemon zest

1 Heat oil in large saucepan; cook onion, stirring, until softened. Add paprika, garlic and chicken; stir to coat chicken in onion mixture.

2 Add stock, juice, chilies, chickpeas and mustard to pan; bring to a boil. Reduce heat; simmer, covered, 30 minutes. Uncover; simmer further 30 minutes or until chicken is tender. Season to taste.

3 Serve chicken sprinkled with parsley and zest.

prep + cook time 1 hour 15 minutes **serves** 4

Chicken in red wine and tomato sauce

  2 tablespoons butter
  2 tablespoons olive oil
  2 white onions, thinly sliced
  2 cloves garlic, crushed
1½ pounds boneless, skinless chicken thighs, halved
  ½ pound button mushrooms, thinly sliced
  1 can (28 ounces) crushed tomatoes
  ¼ cup tomato paste
  ¼ cup dry red wine
  2 teaspoons light brown sugar
  1 teaspoon cracked black peppercorns
  ½ cup chicken stock
  ¼ cup coarsely chopped fresh basil

1 Heat butter and oil in large skillet; cook onion and garlic, stirring, until onion softens. Add chicken; cook, stirring, until browned and almost cooked through.

2 Stir in mushrooms, undrained tomatoes, paste, wine, sugar, peppercorns and stock; bring to the boil. Reduce heat; simmer, uncovered, until chicken is cooked and sauce thickens slightly. Remove from heat; season to taste, stir in basil.

prep + cook time 30 minutes **serves** 4

Grilled lemon thyme chicken

6 cloves garlic, thickly sliced
3 shallots, finely chopped
½ cup chicken stock
2 tablespoons butter, softened
1 tablespoon finely chopped fresh lemon thyme
4 whole chicken legs (about 3 pounds)
1¼ pounds yellow fingerling potatoes, halved lengthways
¾ pound asparagus, trimmed
1 lemon, quartered
1 tablespoon olive oil

1 Place garlic, shallot and stock in small saucepan; bring to a boil. Reduce heat; simmer, uncovered, about 20 minutes or until garlic is soft and liquid is almost evaporated. Cool 5 minutes; stir in butter and thyme.

2 Pat chicken dry with paper towels. Using kitchen scissores, make a pocket between chicken and skin; push thyme mixture under skin.

3 Cook chicken, skin-side down, in heated oiled grill pan, covered, over medium heat, 15 minutes. Turn chicken; cook, covered, about 35 minutes or until cooked through. Cover; stand 15 minutes.

4 Meanwhile, boil, steam or microwave potato until just tender; drain. Cook potato, asparagus and lemon in same grill pan brushing with oil, until browned.

5 Serve chicken with potato, asparagus and lemon.

prep + cook time 1 hour 45 minutes (+ standing) **serves** 4

Honeyed orange quails

  4 quails
  1 tablespoon fresh orange zest
  ½ cup orange juice
1½-inch piece fresh ginger, grated
pinch ground turmeric
  2 tablespoons olive oil
  2 tablespoons honey
  1 teaspoon sweet paprika
  1 orange, cut into 12 wedges
  ½ pound arugula

1 Rinse quails under cold water; pat dry inside and out with paper towels. Discard necks from quails. Using kitchen scissors, cut along each side of each quail's backbone; discard backbones. Skewer each quail lengthways with two skewers.

2 Combine zest, juice, ginger, turmeric, oil, honey and paprika in small bowl.

3 Cook quail in heated oiled grill pan, basting with orange mixture, about 15 minutes or until cooked.

4 Cook orange wedges on heated oiled grill plate for last 10 minutes of quails' cooking time.

5 Serve quail with orange wedges and arugula.

prep + cook time 40 minutes serves 4

Lemon thyme and chili roast chicken

4 small Cornish hens (about 1 pound each)
1 tablespoon fresh lemon thyme

lemon thyme and chili marinade
2 fresh long red chilies, finely chopped
2 cloves garlic, crushed
1 tablespoon fresh lemon thyme
2 teaspoons fresh lemon zest
¼ cup lemon juice
2 tablespoons olive oil
2 tablespoons sherry vinegar
2 tablespoons honey

1 Make lemon thyme and chili marinade.

2 Rinse chickens under cold water; pat dry with absorbent paper. Using kitchen scissors, cut along side of chickens' backbones; discard backbones. Halve chickens along breastbones then cut each half into two pieces.

3 Combine three-quarters of the marinade with chicken in large shallow dish. Cover; refrigerate 3 hours or overnight. Refrigerate remaining marinade until required.

4 Preheat oven to 425°F (400°F convection).

5 Place chicken, in single layer, on wire racks in large shallow baking dishes. Roast about 40 minutes or until cooked.

6 Serve chicken drizzled with reserved marinade and sprinkled with thyme leaves.

lemon thyme and chili marinade Place ingredients in screw-top jar; shake well. Season to taste.

prep + cook time 1 hour 10 minutes (+ refrigeration) **serves** 10

serving suggestion Green salad, steamed green beans, grilled flatbread and lemon wedges.

Chicken phyllo pie

1   pound boneless, skinless chicken breasts, halved
1   pound boneless, skinless chicken thighs, halved
3   cups chicken stock
5   tablespoons butter, chopped
1   small onion, finely chopped
⅓   cup all-purpose flour
6   ounces feta cheese, crumbled
¼   cup each of finely chopped fresh flat-leaf parsley, dill and mint
1   teaspoon ground nutmeg
4   eggs, lightly beaten
8   sheets phyllo pastry
¼   cup olive oil

1 Place chicken and stock in medium saucepan; bring to simmer. Simmer, uncovered, 15 minutes. Remove from heat; cover, stand 15 minutes. Remove chicken from stock. Chop chicken coarsely; strain, reserve 2 cups of the stock. Keep remaining stock for another use.

2 Melt butter in medium saucepan; cook onion, stirring, until onion softens. Add flour; cook, stirring, 1 minute. Gradually stir in hot reserved stock; cook, stirring, over medium heat until mixture boils and thickens. Remove from heat; cool 15 minutes.

3 Preheat oven to 350°F (325°F convection). Oil 10-inch springform pan.

4 Place chicken and sauce mixture in large bowl, combine with cheese, herbs, nutmeg and egg; season.

5 Brush 1 sheet of pastry with oil; top with remaining sheets, brushing each with oil. Line pan with pastry; pour in chicken filling. Roll edges of pastry and tuck down side of pan.

6 Bake pie about 1¼ hours or until browned and set. Stand pie in pan 15 minutes before serving.

prep + cook time 2 hours 10 minutes (+ standing & cooling) **serves** 8

tip Remaining chicken stock can be used in soups, sauces and casseroles. If not using within 3 days, freeze.

serving suggestions Serve warm or cold with green salad.

Meat

Beef kebabs with roasted vegetable salad

2-pound piece beef tenderloin, coarsely chopped
2 tablespoons ras el hanout
½ cup olive oil
3 large red bell peppers
2 red onions, cut into wedges
4 cloves garlic, unpeeled
¼ cup lemon juice
1 tablespoon finely chopped preserved lemon zest
½ teaspoon ground cumin
1 pound roma tomatoes, halved
¼ cup loosley packed fresh cilantro leaves

1 Combine beef, ras el hanout and half the oil in large bowl. Cover; refrigerate 3 hours.

2 Quarter bell peppers; discard seeds and membranes. Cook in heated oiled grill pan, skin-side down, until skin blisters and blackens. Transfer bell peppers to a heatproof bowl; cover with plastic wrap or paper for 5 minutes; peel away skin then chop bell peppers coarsely.

3 Cook onion and garlic in grill plate (or grill or barbecue) until tender; peel away garlic skin, slice garlic thinly.

4 Combine remaining oil, juice, preserved lemon, cumin, tomatoes, bell peppers, onion and garlic in large bowl; season to taste.

5 Thread beef onto six metal skewers. Cook kebabs on heated oiled grill pan until cooked as desired.

6 Sprinkle kebabs with cilantro; serve with roasted veggie salad and, if you like, warm flat bread.

prep + cook time 40 minutes (+ refrigeration) **serves** 6

tip You could substitute beef rump steak for the tenderloin, if you prefer.

Beef kefta with green onion couscous

2 pounds ground beef
1 onion, finely chopped
2 cloves garlic, crushed
2 tablespoons lemon juice
1½ teaspoons each ground coriander and cumin
¼ cup toasted pine nuts
2 tablespoons finely chopped fresh mint
1 tablespoon finely chopped fresh coriander (cilantro)
1 egg
2 cups beef stock
2 cups couscous
2 tablespoons butter
2 scallions, thinly sliced

1 Using hands, combine beef, onion, garlic, juice, spices, nuts, herbs and egg in large bowl, season; roll heaped tablespoons of mixture into balls, thread three balls on each of 12 bamboo skewers. Place kefta skewers on tray, cover; refrigerate 30 minutes.

2 Bring stock to a boil in medium saucepan. Remove from heat, add couscous and butter, cover; stand about 5 minutes or until liquid is absorbed, fluffing with fork occasionally. Stir in scallion; season to taste.

3 Meanwhile, cook kefta in heated oiled grill pan until browned all over and cooked through.

4 Serve kefta with couscous, accompanied by a bowl of combined yogurt and chopped cucumber, if desired.

prep + cook time 35 minutes (+ refrigeration) **serves** 4

tip Soak bamboo skewers in cold water for at least an hour before using to prevent them from burning during cooking.

Moussaka

¼ cup olive oil
2 large eggplants, thinly sliced
1 large onion, finely chopped
2 cloves garlic, crushed
2 pounds ground lamb

1 can (14 ounces) crushed tomatoes
½ cup dry white wine
1 teaspoon ground cinnamon
¼ cup finely grated Pecorino romano cheese

white sauce
5 tablespoons butter
⅓ cup all-purpose flour
2 cups milk

1 Heat oil in large skillet; cook eggplant, in batches, until browned both sides. Drain on absorbent paper towels.

2 Cook onion and garlic in same skillet, stirring, until onion softens. Add lamb; cook, stirring, until lamb changes color. Stir in undrained tomatoes, wine and cinnamon; bring to a boil. Reduce heat; simmer, uncovered, about 30 minutes or until liquid has evaporated.

3 Meanwhile, preheat oven to 350°F (325°F convection). Oil shallow 8-cup rectangular baking dish.

4 Make white sauce.

5 Place one-third of the eggplant, overlapping slices slightly, in dish; spread half the meat sauce over eggplant. Repeat layering with another third of the eggplant, remaining meat sauce and remaining eggplant. Spread white sauce over top layer of eggplant; sprinkle with cheese.

6 Bake moussaka about 40 minutes or until top browns lightly. Cover; stand 10 minutes before serving.

white sauce Melt butter in medium saucepan, add flour; cook, stirring, until mixture bubbles and thickens. Gradually add milk; stir until mixture boils and thickens.

prep + cook time 1 hour 50 minutes **serves** 6
serving suggestion Green salad.

Pastitsio

½ pound macaroni
2 eggs, lightly beaten
¾ cup grated Pecorino romano cheese
2 tablespoons fresh breadcrumbs

½ cup beef stock
¼ cup dry white wine
½ teaspoon ground cinnamon
1 egg, beaten lightly

meat sauce

2 tablespoons olive oil
2 onions, finely chopped
1½ pounds ground lamb
1 can (14 ounces) crushed tomatoes
⅓ cup tomato paste

cheese sauce

6 tablespoons butter
½ cup all-purpose flour
3½ cups milk
1 cup grated Pecorino romano cheese
2 egg yolks

1 Preheat oven to 350°F (325° convection). Oil shallow 10-cup ovenproof dish.

2 Make meat sauce and cheese sauce.

3 Cook pasta in large pot of boiling water until tender; drain. Combine hot pasta, eggs and cheese in large bowl. Press pasta over base of dish.

4 Top pasta evenly with meat sauce; pour over cheese sauce. Smooth surface; sprinkle with breadcrumbs.

5 Bake pastitsio about 1 hour or until lightly browned. Stand 10 minutes before serving.

meat sauce Heat oil in large skillet; cook onion and lamb, stirring, until lamb is browned. Stir in tomato, paste, stock, wine and cinnamon; simmer, uncovered, 20 minutes or until mixture is thick. Cool; stir in egg.

cheese sauce Melt butter in medium saucepan, add flour; cook, stirring, until mixture bubbles and thickens. Remove from heat; gradually stir in milk. Stir over heat until sauce boils and thickens; stir in cheese. Cool 5 minutes; stir in egg yolks.

prep + cook time 2 hours 15 minutes **serves** 6

Veal, quince and caramelized onion tagine

  6 baby brown onions
  6 thick pieces veal knuckle (about 3 pounds)
  2 teaspoons each ground ginger and cinnamon
  ½ teaspoon chili powder
  1 tablespoon olive oil
  1 tablespoon honey
2½ cups beef stock
  3 cloves garlic, crushed
  3 medium quinces, peeled, cored, cut into thick wedges
  ⅓ cup coarsely chopped fresh cilantro

1 Peel onions, leaving root ends intact; halve onions.

2 Combine veal and half the combined spices in large bowl.

3 Heat half the oil in tagine or flameproof casserole dish; cook veal, in batches, until browned. Remove from tagine.

4 Heat remaining oil in same tagine; cook onion, honey and ½ cup of the stock, stirring occasionally, about 5 minutes or until onion caramelizes. Remove from tagine.

5 Add garlic and remaining spices to tagine; cook, stirring, about 1 minute or until fragrant. Return veal to tagine with remaining stock and quince; bring to a boil. Reduce heat; simmer, covered, about 1½ hours or until veal is tender.

6 Add onion to tagine; simmer, covered, about 5 minutes or until heated through. Season to taste.

7 Sprinkle tagine with cilantro and serve with couscous, if you like.

prep + cook time 2 hours 15 minutes **serves** 6

tip Ask your butcher to cut the veal knuckle into 6 thick slices for you. You could use veal shanks if you can't get veal knuckle.

Lamb kebabs with yogurt and pita bread

1 pound ground lamb
1 egg
1 small onion, finely chopped
2 tablespoons finely chopped fresh flat-leaf parsley
1 clove garlic, crushed
2 teaspoons each ground cinnamon and sweet paprika
½ teaspoon cayenne pepper
½ cup yogurt

1 Combine lamb, egg, onion, parsley, garlic and spices in medium bowl. Roll mixture into 16 sausage shapes.

2 Thread sausage shapes onto 16 small bamboo skewers or strong toothpicks; flatten slightly. Cook in heated oiled grill pan until browned and cooked through.

3 Serve kebabs with yogurt.

prep + cook time 30 minutes **makes** 16

tip Soak bamboo skewers in cold water for at least an hour before using to prevent them from scorching during cooking.

serving suggestions Lemon wedges and pita bread.

Lamb kefta

1¼ pounds ground lamb
2 cloves garlic, crushed
1 red onion, finely chopped
1 tablespoon each ground coriander, cumin and sweet paprika
1 cup firmly packed fresh cilantro
2 fresh small red Thai chilies, thinly sliced
2 eggs
1 cup stale breadcrumbs
½ cup beef stock
1 can (28 ounces) diced tomatoes
1 cup sun-dried tomatoes, coarsely chopped
½ cup firmly packed fresh basil, coarsely chopped

1 Preheat oven to 400°F (375°F convection).

2 Combine lamb, garlic, onion, spices, cilantro, chilies, eggs and breadcrumbs in large bowl; season to taste. Roll 2 heaped tablespoons of mixture into balls.

3 Cook meatballs, in batches, in heated oiled flameproof casserole dish, on stove top, until browned. Remove from casserole dish; drain meatballs on paper towels.

4 Return meatballs to tagine with stock, undrained tomatoes, sun-dried tomatoes and basil; bring to a boil.

5 Cover casserole, transfer to oven; cook about 35 minutes or until meatballs are cooked through. Season to taste.

prep + cook time 55 minutes **serves** 4

Stuffed eggplant with lamb and rice

2 large eggplants, halved
¼ cup olive oil
1 onion, finely chopped
¾ pound ground lamb
3 cloves garlic, crushed
⅓ cup medium-grain rice
½ cup water
1 tablespoon lemon juice
2 teaspoons dried oregano
⅔ cup grated Pecorino romano cheese

1 Preheat oven to 425°F (400°F convection).

2 Cut a ½-inch border inside each eggplant; scoop out flesh without breaking skin. Place eggplant shells on oven tray; brush with 1 tablespoon of the oil. Roast about 20 minutes or until tender.

3 Meanwhile, coarsely chop eggplant flesh. Heat 1 tablespoon of the oil in medium skillet; cook eggplant, stirring, until tender. Remove from pan.

4 Heat remaining oil in same pan; cook onion, stirring, until softened. Add lamb; cook, stirring, until browned. Add garlic, cook, stirring, until fragrant. Return eggplant to pan with rice and the water; cook, covered, over low heat, about 10 minutes or until rice is tender. Stir in juice and oregano; season to taste.

5 Spoon lamb mixture into eggplant shells; sprinkle with cheese. Roast about 20 minutes or until cheese is browned.

prep + cook time 1 hour **serves** 4
serving suggestion Greek salad.

Lamb meatballs with egg-lemon sauce

1 tablespoon olive oil
1 onion, finely chopped
1 cup chicken stock
1 pound spinach, trimmed, shredded
2 eggs
1½ tablespoons all-purpose flour
⅓ cup lemon juice

meatballs
1 pound ground lamb
½ cup stale breadcrumbs
½ cup grated Parmesean cheese
1 tablespoon finely chopped fresh dill
1 egg
2 teaspoons fresh lemon zest

1 Make meatballs.

2 Heat oil in deep skillet; cook meatballs until browned. Remove from pan.

3 Cook onion in same pan, stirring, until softened. Return meatballs to pan with stock; bring to a boil. Reduce heat; simmer, covered, about 15 minutes or until meatballs are cooked through. Reserve ½ cup of hot cooking liquid. Stir spinach into pan, cook until wilted. Remove pan from heat.

4 Meanwhile, beat eggs with fork in medium bowl until combined; whisk in flour and juice. Whisk in reserved hot liquid; stir mixture into meatballs. Stir gently until mixture simmers; season to taste.

meatballs Combine ingredients in large bowl; season. Roll rounded tablespoons of mixture into balls.

prep + cook time 45 minutes **serves** 4

serving suggestions Arugala salad and crusty bread.

Baked lamb shanks with orzo

1 tablespoon olive oil
4 French-trimmed lamb shanks (about 8 ounces each)
1 onion, finely chopped
3 cinnamon sticks
1 bay leaf
3 cloves garlic, crushed
1 can (14 ounces) diced tomatoes
2 cups chicken stock
1¼ cups orzo
1 cup water
2 tablespoons fresh oregano

1 Preheat oven to 400°F (375°F convection).

2 Heat oil in large baking dish; cook lamb over medium heat until browned all over. Remove from dish.

3 Cook onion, cinnamon and bay leaf in same dish, stirring, until onion softens. Add garlic; cook, stirring, until fragrant. Return lamb to dish with undrained tomatoes and stock; bring to a boil. Cover dish with lid or foil; cook in oven 1¼ hours.

4 Stir orzo and the water into dish; cook, covered, about 30 minutes or until lamb and orzo are tender. Season to taste.

5 Serve lamb sprinkled with oregano.

prep + cook time 2 hours 10 minutes **serves** 4

tip You can replace orzo with risoni if you like. Orzo, like risoni, absorbs cooking liquid. If the sauce is too thick, stir in a little extra water. If you make this dish in advance, you will need to add some water or stock when reheating.

Honeyed lamb shanks

8 French-trimmed lamb shanks (about 3 pounds)
2 tablespoons all-purpose flour
¼ cup olive oil
2 onions, coarsely chopped
3 cloves garlic, crushed
1 teaspoon ground cinnamon
2 teaspoons each ground cumin and coriander
1 cup dry red wine
4 cups chicken stock
2 tablespoons honey
2 small sweet potato, coarsely chopped

1 Preheat oven to 350°F (325°F convection).

2 Toss lamb in flour; shake away excess. Heat 2 tablespoons of the oil in large flameproof casserole dish on stovetop; cook lamb, in batches, until browned, drain on paper towels.

3 Heat remaining oil in same dish; cook onion, garlic and spices, stirring, until onion softens and mixture is fragrant. Add wine; bring to a boil. Reduce heat; simmer, uncovered, about 5 minutes or until liquid reduces by half.

4 Add stock and honey to dish; bring to a boil. Return lamb to dish; cook, covered, in oven about 1½ hours, turning shanks occasionally. Uncover dish, add sweet potatoes; cook, uncovered, about 50 minutes or until sweet potatoes are just tender and lamb is almost falling off the bone. Transfer lamb and sweet potatoes to platter; cover to keep warm.

5 Place dish with pan juices over high heat on stovetop; bring to a boil. Boil, uncovered, about 15 minutes or until sauce thickens slightly, season to taste.

6 Serve shanks with couscous, if desired.

prep + cook time 3 hours 15 minutes **serves** 4

Slow-roasted spiced lamb shoulder

 2 teaspoons fennel seeds
 1 teaspoon each ground cinnamon, ginger and cumin
 ¼ teaspoon chili powder
 2 tablespoons olive oil
2½-pound lamb shoulder, shank intact
 2 cloves garlic, thinly sliced
 6 baby brown onions
 ¾ pound baby carrots, trimmed
 1 cup water

1 Preheat oven to 350°F (325°F convection).

2 Toast spices in small dry skillet until fragrant. Combine spices and half the oil in small bowl.

3 Using sharp knife, score lamb at 1-inch intervals; push garlic into cuts. Rub lamb all over with spice mixture, season.

4 Heat remaining oil in large flameproof dish; cook lamb, turning, until browned all over. Remove lamb from dish.

5 Meanwhile, peel onions, leaving root ends intact. Add onions to dish; cook, stirring, until browned.

6 Add carrots and the water to dish, bring to a boil; top with lamb, cover loosely with foil. Transfer to oven; roast 1½ hours.

7 Reduce oven to 325°F (300°F convection).

8 Uncover lamb; roast a further 1½ hours or until lamb is tender. Cover lamb; stand 10 minutes, then slice thinly. Strain pan juices into small heatproof bowl.

9 Serve lamb with onions, carrots and pan juices; accompany with steamed green beans, if desired.

prep + cook time 3 hours 30 minutes **serves** 4

Paprika pork chops with carrot and olive salad

2 tablespoons olive oil
¼ cup lemon juice
2 teaspoons ground cumin
1 tablespoon sweet paprika
4 pork chops (8 ounces each)

carrot and olive salad
4 carrots, halved lengthways, thinly sliced
1 cup pitted black olives, coarsely chopped
½ cup loosely packed fresh flat-leaf parsley
½ cup loosely packed fresh cilantro
2 tablespoons olive oil
2 teaspoons ground cumin
1 tablespoon red wine vinegar

1 Combine oil, juice, cumin, paprika and pork in large bowl, season.

2 Cook pork in heated oiled grill pan until cooked as desired.

3 Meanwhile, make carrot and olive salad.

4 Serve pork with salad.

carrot and olive salad Boil, steam or microwave carrot until tender; drain. Cool 10 minutes. Place carrot in medium bowl with remaining ingredients; toss gently to combine.

prep + cook time 30 minutes **serves** 4

Spiced pork skewers with orange honey glaze

1 pound pork tenderloin
2 cloves garlic, crushed
2 teaspoons cumin seeds
½ teaspoon ground coriander
¼ teaspoon sweet paprika
1 tablespoon olive oil

orange honey glaze
½ cup orange juice
2 tablespoons honey
2 tablespoons barbecue sauce
1 teaspoon Dijon mustard

1 Cut pork into 1-inch pieces. Combine pork, garlic, seeds, spices and oil in medium bowl; season.

2 Thread pork onto eight bamboo skewers.

3 Cook skewers in heated oiled grill pan until browned and cooked through.

4 Meanwhile, make orange honey glaze.

5 Serve skewers with glaze.

orange honey glaze Stir ingredients in small saucepan over heat until boiling. Reduce heat; simmer, uncovered, about 5 minutes or until thickened.

prep + cook time 30 minutes **makes** 8

tip Soak skewers in water for at least 1 hour before using, to avoid scorching during cooking.

Vegetarian

Eggplant, tomato and chickpea casserole

2 eggplants, thickly sliced
2 tablespoons olive oil
¼ pound green beans, trimmed, halved
10 spring onions (about ½ pound), trimmed
2 cloves garlic, crushed
3 stalks celery, trimmed, thinly sliced
2 cans (15 ounces) chickpeas, rinsed, drained
4 large tomatoes, peeled, finely chopped
¼ cup each finely chopped fresh flat-leaf parsley and oregano
1 tablespoon tomato paste

1 Preheat oven to 350°F (325°F convection). Preheat broiler.

2 Place eggplant slices on oiled baking sheet; brush lightly with half the oil. Place under broiler until browned both sides.

3 Meanwhile, boil, steam or microwave beans until tender; drain.

4 Heat remaining oil in large flameproof casserole dish; cook onion, stirring, until browned lightly. Stir in eggplant, garlic, celery, chickpeas, tomato and herbs. Cook, covered, in oven 45 minutes or until vegetables are tender. Remove from oven; stir in paste and beans.

prep + cook time 1 hour 20 minutes **serves** 4

serving suggestions Warmed crusty bread and yogurt.

Braised borlotti beans with tomato and garlic

  1 pound fresh borlotti beans, shelled
⅓ cup olive oil
  1 cup water
  1 bulb garlic, cut in half horizontally
  3 large ripe tomatoes, coarsely chopped
¼ cup fresh oregano
½ cup coarsely chopped fresh basil

1 Preheat oven to 350°F (325°F convection).

2 Place beans in medium baking dish; drizzle with oil and the water. Add garlic, tomato and oregano; bake, covered, about 1¼ hours or until beans are tender. Stir in basil.

prep + cook time 1 hour 25 minutes **serves** 4

Fava beans and artichokes

2 pounds fresh or frozen fava beans
1 can (14 ounces) artichokes, drained, halved

tomato dressing
1 tomato, seeded, finely chopped
2 tablespoons finely shredded fresh basil
2 tablespoons olive oil
1 tablespoon white wine vinegar

1 Make tomato dressing.

2 Add shelled fava beans to pot of boiling salted water, boil, uncovered, about 2 minutes or until skins wrinkle; drain. Transfer to bowl of iced water, stand 2 minutes; drain. Peel fava beans; discard shell.

3 Place beans in medium bowl with artichokes and dressing; toss gently to combine. Season to taste.

tomato dressing Combine ingredients in small bowl; season to taste.

prep + cook time 20 minutes **serves** 4

tip You will need about 2 pounds fresh fava beans for this recipe.

Braised green beans

½ pound Swiss chard
1 tablespoon olive oil
1 small onion, thinly sliced
2 cloves garlic, thinly sliced
1 fresh small red chili, thinly sliced
8 baby potatoes, quartered
½ pound baby green beans, trimmed
1 can (14 ounces) chopped tomatoes

1 Wash and dry Swiss chard; chop leaves and stems.

2 Heat oil in medium heavy-based saucepan; cook Swiss chard stems, onion, garlic and chili, stirring, about 10 minutes or until stems soften.

3 Add potato and undrained tomatoes; simmer, covered, 15 minutes. Add beans; cook about 5 minutes until potato is tender. Season to taste.

4 Just before serving, add Swiss chard leaves; cook about 3 minutes or until wilted.

prep + cook time 45 minutes **serves** 6 as a side

Vegetable tagine

1 tablespoon each coriander seeds, cumin seeds and caraway seeds
1 tablespoon vegetable oil
3 cloves garlic, crushed
2 large onions, finely chopped
2 teaspoons each sweet paprika and ground ginger
1 tablespoon tomato paste
2 cups water
1 can (28 ounces) canned diced tomatoes
1¼ pounds butternut squash, coarsely chopped

8 yellow patty pan squash, quartered
½ pound baby green beans, trimmed, halved
1 can (15 ounces) canned chickpeas, rinsed, drained

lemon couscous
2 cups couscous
2 cups boiling water
2 teaspoons fresh lemon zest
2 teaspoons lemon juice
2 tablespoons coarsely chopped fresh flat-leaf parsley

1 Using mortar and pestle, crush seeds to a fine powder. Sift into small bowl; discard husks.

2 Heat oil in tagine or large pot; cook garlic and onion, stirring, until onion softens. Add crushed seeds and spices; cook, stirring, until fragrant.

3 Add paste, the water, undrained tomatoes and butternut squash; bring to a boil. Reduce heat; simmer, uncovered, 20 minutes. Stir in patty pan squash, beans and chickpeas; simmer, covered, about 10 minutes or until vegetables are tender, season to taste.

4 Meanwhile, make lemon couscous.

5 Serve tagine with couscous.

lemon couscous Combine couscous with the water in large heatproof bowl, cover; stand about 5 minutes or until liquid is absorbed, fluffing with fork occasionally. Stir in zest, juice and parsley.

prep + cook time 1 hour 5 minutes **serves** 6

Spicy lentil and rice salad

1 cup basmati rice
1 cup brown lentils
¼ cup olive oil
2 tablespoons butter
4 red onions, thinly sliced
4 cloves garlic, crushed
2 teaspoons each ground cilantro, cinnamon, cumin and sweet paprika
4 scallions, thinly sliced

1 Cook rice and lentils in medium saucepan of boiling water until tender; drain. Rinse under cold water; drain.

2 Meanwhile, heat oil and butter in large frying pan; cook red onion and garlic, stirring occasionally, about 20 minutes or until onion is lightly caramelized.

3 Add spices; cook, stirring, about 1 minute or until fragrant.

4 Remove from heat; stir in scallions, rice, and lentils. Season to taste. Serve warm.

prep + cook time 35 minutes **serves** 6

Sweet and spicy vegetable tagine

2 tablespoons olive oil
1 onion, thinly sliced
2-inch piece fresh ginger, grated
2 cloves garlic, crushed
2 teaspoons each ground coriander and cumin
1 teaspoon sweet paprika
1 pound butternut squash, coarsely chopped
1 medium sweet potato, coarsely chopped
2 small parsnips, coarsely chopped
2 cups vegetable stock
1 can (14 ounces) diced tomatoes
2 tablespoons honey
8 small yellow patty pan squash, halved
¾ pound baby carrots, trimmed
⅓ cup raisins
2 tablespoons finely chopped fresh flat-leaf parsley
¼ cup flaked almonds, toasted

1 Heat oil in tagine or flameproof casserole dish; cook onion, stirring, until softened. Add ginger, garlic and spices; cook, stirring, about 1 minute or until fragrant.

2 Add butternut squash, sweet potato, parsnip, stock, undrained tomatoes and honey; bring to a boil. Reduce heat; simmer, covered, 15 minutes. Add patty pan squash and carrots; simmer, uncovered, 20 minutes or until vegetables are tender, season to taste.

3 Stir in raisins and parsley; sprinkle with nuts.

prep + cook time 55 minutes **serves** 8

White beans and lentils

1 tablespoon olive oil
1 onion, coarsely chopped
2 cloves garlic, crushed
1- inch piece fresh ginger, cut into matchsticks
1 teaspoon harissa
1 can (28 ounces) whole peeled tomatoes, coarsely chopped
1 medium red bell pepper, coarsely chopped
2 cups water
1 can (15 ounces) white beans, rinsed, drained
¾ cup brown lentils, rinsed, drained
¼ cup finely chopped fresh mint
¼ cup finely chopped fresh flat-leaf parsley

1 Heat oil in tagine or large skillet; cook onion, stirring, until softened. Add garlic, ginger and harissa; cook, stirring, about 1 minute or until fragrant.

2 Add undrained tomatoes, bell peppers, the water, beans and lentils; bring to a boil. Reduce heat; simmer, uncovered, about 25 minutes or until lentils are soft. Remove from heat; stir in mint, season to taste.

3 Serve tagine sprinkled with parsley; accompany with grilled flatbread, if you like.

prep + cook time 40 minutes **serves** 4

tip We used cannellini beans in this recipe but you can use any canned white beans you like.

Vegetable kebabs

12 shallots, peeled
½ pound cherry tomatoes
2 zucchini, cut into six pieces each
12 baby beets, trimmed
36 fresh bay leaves

dressing
2 cloves garlic, crushed
¼ cup dukkah
1 tablespoon fresh lemon zest
½ cup olive oil

1 Make dressing.

2 Combine shallots, tomatoes, zucchini and half the dressing in large bowl.

3 Place beets in medium saucepan, cover with cold water; bring to a boil. Boil 15 minutes; drain, cool. Using disposable gloves, squeeze skins from each beet.

4 Thread shallots, tomatoes, zucchini, beets and bay leaves onto 12 metal skewers.

5 Cook kebabs on heated oiled grill pan about 15 minutes or until vegetables are tender. Season to taste.

6 Serve kebabs drizzled with remaining dressing and yogurt, if desired.

dressing Place ingredients in screw-top jar; shake well.

prep + cook time 40 minutes **makes** 12

tip Cut vegetables the same size for even cooking. If you have time, the shallot mixture will develop more flavor if it's covered and refrigerated overnight.

Moroccan-style vegetables

  2 tablespoons olive oil
  2 large onions, thickly sliced
  2 cloves garlic, crushed
  2 teaspoons ground coriander
  1 teaspoon each ground cumin and sweet paprika
  2 cinnamon sticks
pinch ground saffron
  2 fresh small red Thai chilies, finely chopped
  2 baby eggplant, coarsely chopped
1½ pounds butternut squash, coarsely chopped
  1 can (15 ounces) tomatoes
  1 cup vegetable stock
  2 cups water
  1 can (15 ounces) chickpeas, rinsed, drained
  2 large zucchini, coarsely chopped
 ½ cup loosely packed fresh coriander (cilantro) leaves
  1 tablespoon lemon juice

1 Heat oil in large, deep skillet; cook onion and garlic, stirring, until onion softens. Add spices, chilies and eggplant; cook, stirring, until fragrant.

2 Add squash, undrained tomatoes, stock, water and chickpeas; bring to a boil. Reduce heat; simmer, covered, 10 minutes. Add zucchini; simmer, covered, about 5 minutes or until vegetables are tender.

3 Stir cilantro and juice into vegetable mixture, season to taste; serve with steamed couscous.

prep + cook time 35 minutes **serves** 4

Vegetable paella

    1 tablespoon olive oil
    1 small red onion, finely chopped
    1 red bell pepper, finely chopped
    1 yellow bell pepper, finely chopped
    1 teaspoon smoked paprika
    ½ pound brown mushrooms, halved
1⅔ cups brown short-grain rice
pinch saffron threads
    4 tomatoes, coarsely chopped
    4 cups vegetable stock
    ½ pound green beans, trimmed, coarsely chopped
    1 cup frozen peas
    2 tablespoons coarsely chopped fresh flat-leaf parsley
    1 lemon, cut into wedges

1 Heat oil in large deep skillet; cook onion and bell peppers, stirring, until onion softens. Add paprika and mushrooms; cook, stirring, until mushrooms are tender. Add rice and saffron; stir to coat rice in vegetable mixture.

2 Add tomato and 1 cup of the stock; cook, stirring, until liquid is absorbed. Add remaining stock; cook, covered, stirring occasionally, about 1 hour or until liquid is absorbed and rice is tender.

3 Sprinkle beans and peas over rice (do not stir to combine). Cook, covered, about 10 minutes or until beans are tender. Season to taste.

4 Cover paella; stand 5 minutes. Sprinkle paella with parsley; serve with lemon wedges.

prep + cook time 1 hour 40 minutes **serves** 6

Stuffed peppers

2 teaspoons olive oil
1 red onion, finely chopped
1 tablespoon slivered almonds
⅔ cup white long-grain rice
1 cup water
2 tablespoons finely chopped
  dried apricots
¼ cup sun-dried tomatoes, finely
  chopped
¼ cup finely chopped fresh flat-leaf
  parsley
4 red bell peppers
  cooking-oil spray

roasted tomato salad
2 tomatoes, cut into thick wedges
1 tablespoon cider vinegar
½ teaspoon cracked black pepper
1 teaspoon sugar
1 cup firmly packed fresh flat-leaf
  parsley leaves
½ cup firmly packed fresh mint

1 Preheat oven to 400°F (375°F convection).

2 Heat oil in medium saucepan; cook onion and nuts, stirring, until onion softens. Add rice; cook, stirring, 1 minute. Add the water; bring to a boil. Reduce heat; simmer, covered, 15 minutes or until liquid is absorbed and rice is tender. Stir in apricot, tomato and parsley; season to taste.

3 Carefully cut tops off bell peppers; discard tops. Discard seeds and membranes, leaving bell peppers intact. Spoon rice mixture into bell peppers; place bell peppers on baking sheet, spray with oil. Roast 10 minutes. Cover loosely with foil; roast about 20 minutes or until bell peppers are just soft.

4 Meanwhile, make roasted tomato salad.

5 Serve bell peppers with roasted tomato salad.

roasted tomato salad Combine tomato, vinegar, pepper and sugar in medium bowl. Drain; reserve liquid. Place tomato on baking sheet; roast, alongside bell peppers, 10 minutes or until tomato just softens. Place tomato and reserved liquid in medium bowl with herbs; toss gently to combine.

prep + cook time 1 hour 15 minutes **serves** 4

Cheese and tomato tortilla

4 scallions, thickly sliced
1 red bell pepper, coarsely chopped
2 cloves garlic, crushed
1 fresh long red chili, finely chopped
2 tomatoes, coarsely chopped
6 ounces feta cheese, crumbled
8 eggs
1¼ cups heavy cream
¼ cup firmly packed fresh flat-leaf parsley leaves, coarsely chopped

1 Heat oiled 10-inch skillet; cook onion, bell pepper, garlic and chili, stirring, until vegetables are tender. Remove from heat; stir in tomato and cheese.

2 Whisk eggs, cream and parsley in large bowl, season. Pour over vegetable mixture; stir gently.

3 Preheat broiler.

4 Return pan to low heat; cook tortilla, uncovered, until just set. Place pan under broiler to brown tortilla top. Cut into wedges to serve.

prep + cook time 35 minutes **serves** 4

tip Wrap the handle of your skillet with foil to protect it, if necessary.

Sweets and
Drinks

Spiced oranges with brown sugar toffee

    1 cup firmly packed light brown sugar
    1 cup water
    3 oranges, peeled, thickly sliced
    3 medium blood oranges, peeled, thickly sliced
    ¼ teaspoon ground cinnamon
pinch ground cardamom
    1 teaspoon orange blossom water

1 Stir sugar and the water in medium saucepan over medium heat until sugar dissolves; bring to a boil. Boil, uncovered, without stirring, about 10 minutes or until mixture is a dark caramel color. Remove from heat; allow bubbles to subside.

2 Meanwhile, arrange orange slices, overlapping slightly, on large heatproof platter; sprinkle with spices and orange blossom water.

3 Pour half the toffee over oranges; pour remaining toffee onto greased baking sheet. Stand oranges at room temperature about 2 hours or until toffee dissolves and forms a sauce over oranges. Allow toffee on tray to set at room temperature.

4 Break set toffee into pieces; sprinkle over oranges.

prep + cook time 25 minutes (+ standing) **serves** 6

tip When you think the syrup has almost reached the color we suggest, quickly remove the pan from the heat, remembering that the syrup will continue to cook and darken during this time. Let the bubbles subside, then drop a teaspoon of the syrup into a cup of cold water. The toffee should set the instant it hits the cold water; lift it out and break it with your fingers. If the toffee needs to be harder, then return the mixture to the heat and cook a little more. This test is easy, but a candy thermometer removes all the guess work for you. If you have a candy thermometer, boil the mixture until it reaches 280°F.

Fresh peaches and dates with orange blossom water

½ cup sugar
pinch saffron threads
4 cardamom pods
½ cup water
⅓ cup lemon juice
1 teaspoon orange blossom water
6 large peaches, thickly sliced
12 fresh dates, pitted, quartered
1 cup Greek-style yogurt

1 Stir sugar, saffron, cardamom and the water in small saucepan over low heat, until sugar dissolves. Bring to a boil. Reduce heat; simmer, uncovered, about 5 minutes or until syrup thickens slightly. Cool 10 minutes. Stir in juice and orange blossom water.

2 Place peaches and dates in large bowl; strain syrup over fruit. Cover; refrigerate 2 hours.

3 Serve fruit with yogurt.

prep + cook time 15 minutes (+ refrigeration) **serves** 8

Melon salad with citrus sugar

½ large pineapple, peeled, thinly sliced
½ medium cantaloupe, peeled, thinly sliced
2½-pound piece seedless watermelon, peeled, thinly sliced
2 oranges, peeled, thinly sliced

citrus sugar
⅓ cup sugar
1 tablespoon fresh orange zest
2 teaspoons fresh lime zest
1 tablespoon finely chopped fresh mint

1 Make citrus sugar.

2 Just before serving, layer fruit on large serving platter, sprinkling citrus sugar between layers.

3 Serve with extra mint leaves, if desired.

citrus sugar Process ingredients until combined.

prep time 20 minutes **serves** 6

Cherry spoon sweet

1   can (14 ounces) pitted dark cherries in syrup
1   cup sugar
1   vanilla bean, split lengthways
2   (2-inch) strips lemon zest
1   teaspoon lemon juice

1 Drain cherries over small saucepan; reserve cherries.

2 Add sugar, vanilla bean, zest and juice to pan; stir over heat until sugar dissolves.

3 Add reserved cherries, bring to a boil; boil, uncovered, about 7 minutes or until mixture thickens and will coat the back of a metal spoon. Cool to room temperature.

prep + cook time 15 minutes (+ cooling) **serves** 6

serving suggestion This is traditionally served with a glass of cold water when guests arrive.

Figs in orange syrup with yogurt cream

2   oranges
1   cup sugar
1   cup water
½   cup honey
2   cinnamon sticks
1   vanilla bean
1   tablespoon orange blossom water
8   large fresh figs, halved

yogurt cream
¾   cup greek-style yogurt
½   cup heavy cream

1 Using vegetable peeler, remove 8 wide strips of zest from each orange. Remove any white pith from zest.

2 Place zest strips, sugar, the water, honey and cinnamon in small saucepan. Split vanilla bean; scrape seeds into pan with bean. Stir over low heat until sugar dissolves; bring to a boil. Reduce heat; simmer, uncovered, about 10 minutes or until syrup thickens slightly. Remove from heat; stir in orange blossom water.

3 Place figs, cut-side up, in large heatproof dish. Pour hot syrup over figs; cool.

4 Meanwhile, make yogurt cream.

5 Serve figs with yogurt cream.

yogurt cream Combine ingredients in small bowl. Cover; refrigerate until serving.

prep + cook time 20 minutes (+ cooling) **serves** 8

Rice pudding with cinnamon and vanilla

3 cups milk
¼ cup sugar
2 (2-inch) strips lemon zest
1 vanilla bean, split lengthways
1 cinnamon stick
⅓ cup white medium-grain rice
3 egg yolks
⅓ cup walnuts, roasted, coarsely chopped
¼ teaspoon ground cinnamon

1 Combine milk, sugar and zest in medium saucepan; bring to a boil, stirring occasionally. Add vanilla bean and cinnamon stick, gradually stir in rice; cook, covered tightly, over low heat, stirring occasionally, about 40 minutes or until rice is tender. Discard zest, cinnamon stick and vanilla bean.

2 Combine 1 tablespoon of the hot milk mixture with egg yolks in small heatproof bowl. Pour egg yolk mixture into rice, stirring over low heat, until mixture thickens.

3 Serve pudding sprinkled with nuts and ground cinnamon.

prep + cook time 55 minutes **serves** 4

tip This dish can be served warm or cooled.

Saffron panna cotta with honeyed figs

1 cup heavy cream
½ cup sugar
pinch saffron threads
8 cardamom pods, bruised
2 cinnamon sticks
4 teaspoons gelatin
2 tablespoons water
2 cups buttermilk

honeyed figs
¼ cup honey
¼ cup dry red wine
⅓ cup finely chopped dried figs

1 Stir cream, sugar and spices in medium saucepan over low heat until sugar dissolves. Bring to a boil. Strain mixture into large glass measuring cup; cool 5 minutes.

2 Meanwhile, sprinkle gelatin over the water in small heatproof bowl. Stand bowl in small saucepan of simmering water; stir until gelatin dissolves, cool 5 minutes.

3 Stir gelatin mixture and buttermilk into cream mixture. Divide mixture into six ¾-cup molds. Cover; refrigerate 4 hours or until set.

4 Make honeyed figs.

5 Turn panna cottas onto serving plates; top with honeyed figs.

honeyed figs Bring ingredients to a boil in medium saucepan. Reduce heat; simmer, uncovered, about 5 minutes or until syrup thickens slightly. Cool.

prep + cook time 30 minutes (+ refrigeration) **serves** 6

Spiced crème caramel

¾ cup sugar
½ cup water
1¼ cups heavy cream
1¾ cups milk
4 cardamom pods, bruised
¼ teaspoon saffron threads
2 teaspoons rosewater
6 eggs
⅓ cup sugar, extra

1 Stir sugar and the water in medium skillet over medium heat until sugar dissolves; bring to a boil. Boil, uncovered, without stirring, until mixture is a dark caramel color. Remove from heat; allow bubbles to subside. Pour toffee into deep 8-inch round cake pan.

2 Bring cream, milk, spices and rosewater to a boil in medium saucepan. Remove from heat; stand 30 minutes, then return to a boil.

3 Whisk eggs and extra sugar in medium bowl; whisking constantly, pour hot milk mixture into egg mixture. Strain mixture into cake pan; discard solids.

4 Meanwhile, preheat oven to 325°F (300°F convection).

5 Place pan in medium baking dish; add enough boiling water to come half way up side of pan. Bake about 40 minutes or until set. Remove pan from baking dish. Cover crème caramel; refrigerate overnight.

6 Gently ease crème caramel from side of pan; invert onto deep-sided serving plate.

prep + cook time 1 hour (+ standing & refrigeration) **serves** 6

Cinnamon flan

　1　cup sugar
　½　cup water
2½　cups milk
1¼　cups heavy cream
　2　cinnamon sticks
　2　cloves
　4　eggs
　2　egg yolks
　⅓　cup sugar, extra
　2　teaspoons vanilla extract

1 Preheat oven to 325°F (300°F convection).

2 Stir sugar and the water in medium saucepan over low heat until sugar dissolves; bring to a boil. Reduce heat; simmer, uncovered, without stirring, until mixture is golden brown in color. Pour toffee into deep 8-inch round cake pan. Place pan in large baking dish.

3 Bring milk, cream and spices to a boil in medium saucepan. Remove from heat; stand, covered, 15 minutes. Strain milk mixture into large heatproof bowl; discard spices.

4 Whisk eggs, egg yolks, extra sugar and extract in medium bowl. Gradually whisk milk mixture into egg mixture; strain mixture over toffee in pan. Add enough boiling water to baking dish to come halfway up side of pan. Bake about 45 minutes or until custard sets. Remove pan from water; cool. Cover; refrigerate 24 hours.

5 Just before serving, turn flan onto a rimmed serving dish.

prep + cook time 1 hour 15 minutes (+ standing & refrigeration) **serves** 8

tip This recipe must be made 24 hours in advance to allow the toffee to dissolve.

Galaktoboureko

5 cups milk	1 tablespoon sugar
1¾ cups sugar	¼ teaspoon ground cinnamon
1 vanilla bean, split lengthways	
1 cup fine semolina	**lemon syrup**
2 tablespoons butter	1 cup sugar
4 eggs	¾ cup water
16 sheets frozen phyllo pastry, thawed	2 (2 inch) strips lemon zest
10 tablespoons butter, melted	2 teaspoons lemon juice

1 Stir milk, sugar and vanilla bean in large saucepan over heat until sugar dissolves; bring to a boil. Gradually whisk semolina into milk mixture; whisk over medium heat about 5 minutes or until thickened.

2 Remove pan from heat; discard vanilla bean. Stir in butter. Transfer custard to large heatproof bowl; cover surface of custard with plastic wrap. Cool 1 hour. Stir in eggs.

3 Preheat oven to 325°F (300°F convection). Coat a 9 x 13-inch baking dish with cooking oil spray.

4 Cut pastry sheets to the same size as dish; discard excess pastry. Brush 1 sheet of pastry with some of the butter; top with 7 more pastry sheets, brushing each with butter. Place in base of dish; spread custard into dish. Repeat with remaining pastry and butter; place on top of custard.

5 Bake galaktoboureko about 55 minutes or until custard is set.

6 Meanwhile, make lemon syrup.

7 Pour hot syrup over hot galaktoboureko; cool. Serve dusted with combined confectioners' sugar and cinnamon.

lemon syrup Stir ingredients in small saucepan over heat until sugar dissolves; bring to a boil. Reduce heat; simmer, uncovered, 10 minutes or until thickened slightly. Discard rind.

prep + cook time 1 hour 40 minutes (+ cooling) **makes** 21

Loukoumades

    1 cup warm water
1½ teaspoons dry yeast
    1 teaspoon sugar
 ½ teaspoon salt
1½ cups all-purpose flour
vegetable oil, for deep-frying
    1 teaspoon ground cinnamon

honey citrus syrup
    1 cup honey
 ½ cup sugar
 ½ cup water
    2 (2-inch) strips lemon zest
    2 (2-inch) strips orange zest

1 Whisk the water, yeast, sugar and salt together in small bowl until yeast is dissolved.

2 Sift flour into large bowl; gradually stir in yeast mixture until smooth. Cover; stand in warm place about 45 minutes or until mixture has doubled in size.

3 Meanwhile, make honey citrus syrup.

4 Heat oil in large saucepan or wok; deep-fry rounded teaspoons of batter, in batches, until lightly browned and cooked through. Drain on paper towels.

5 Drizzle hot loukoumades with syrup, sprinkle with cinnamon. Serve loukoumades warm.

honey citrus syrup Stir ingredients in small saucepan over heat until sugar dissolves; bring to a boil. Reduce heat; simmer, 10 minutes or until slightly thickened. Cool.

prep + cook time 35 minutes (+ standing) **makes** 36

Orange shortbread cookies

½ cup roasted unsalted shelled pistachios
2 sticks butter, chopped
1 cup confectioners' sugar
1½ cups all-purpose flour
2 tablespoons cornstarch
¾ cup ground almonds
2 tablespoons orange blossom water
⅓ cup confectioners' sugar, extra

1 Preheat oven to 300°F (275°F convection). Line two baking sheets with parchment paper.

2 Finely chop ⅓ cup of the pistachios, leave remaining pistachios whole.

3 Beat butter and confectioners' sugar in small bowl with electric mixer until combined. Transfer mixture to large bowl; stir in sifted flours, ground almonds and chopped pistachios.

4 Shape level tablespoons of mixture into mounds about 1 inch apart on baking sheets, press a whole pistachio on each.

5 Bake cookies about 25 minutes or until firm. Transfer cookies to wire racks, brush with orange blossom water; stand 5 minutes. Dust cookies with extra sifted icing sugar; cool.

prep + cook time 50 minutes **makes** 40

Honey walnut cookies

1 cup vegetable oil
½ cup sugar
½ cup orange juice
2 tablespoons brandy
1 egg
4 cups self-rising flour
1 cup fine semolina
1 teaspoon ground cinnamon
1 cup walnut pieces, finely chopped

spiced syrup
1 cup sugar
½ cup honey
½ cup water
2 tablespoons lemon juice
1 cinnamon stick
6 cloves

1 Preheat oven to 325°F (300°F convection). Line baking sheets with parchment paper.

2 Combine oil, sugar, juice, brandy and egg in large bowl. Stir in sifted flour, semolina and half the cinnamon.

3 Roll level tablespoons of mixture into 2½-inch oval shapes. Place on sheets, about 1½ inches apart.

4 Bake cookies about 25 minutes. Cool on sheets.

5 Meanwhile, make spiced syrup.

6 Dip cookies, in batches, into hot syrup for about 30 seconds or until well coated; transfer to wire rack. Sprinkle cookies with combined walnuts and remaining cinnamon. Cool.

spiced syrup Stir ingredients in small saucepan over heat until sugar dissolves; bring to a boil. Reduce heat; simmer, uncovered, about 7 minutes or until slightly thickened. Strain into heatproof bowl.

prep + cook time 55 minutes (+ cooling) **makes** 48

Baklava

1½ cups shelled unsalted pistachio nuts
 2 cups walnut pieces
¼ cup sugar
 2 tablespoons fine semolina
 1 teaspoon ground cinnamon
pinch ground cloves
 12 ounces frozen phyllo pastry dough,
    thawed
1¼ cups (2½ sticks) butter, melted
 30 whole cloves

syrup
 1 cup sugar
 1 cup water
¼ cup honey
 1 tablespoon lemon juice
 1 cinnamon stick

1 Preheat oven to 400°F (375°F convection). Coat a 9 x 13 baking pan with cooking oil
   spray.

2 Process nuts, sugar, semolina, cinnamon and ground cloves until chopped finely; transfer
   to medium bowl.

3 Brush 1 sheet of pastry with a little of the butter; top with 7 more sheets, brushing each
   well with butter. Fold pastry in half, place into pan. Sprinkle pastry with thin even layer of
   the nut mixture. Layer another 2 sheets of pastry, brushing each well with more butter.
   Fold pastry in half, place in pan; top with another layer of nut mixture. Repeat layering
   process until all nut mixture has been used. Repeat layering and buttering with any
   remaining pastry sheets; brush the final layer with butter. Score the top lightly in
   diamond pattern; press one whole clove into center of each piece.

4 Bake baklava about 50 minutes.

5 Meanwhile, make syrup.

6 Pour syrup over hot baklava. Cool before cutting.

syrup Stir ingredients in small saucepan over heat until sugar dissolves; bring to the boil.
Reduce heat; simmer, uncovered, about 10 minutes or until slightly thickened. Discard
cinnamon; cool syrup.

prep + cook time 1 hour 20 minutes (+ cooling) **makes** 30

Fig galettes

1 sheet frozen puff pastry, thawed
⅓ cup ground almonds
4 large fresh figs, thinly sliced
2 tablespoons butter, melted
2 tablespoons pure maple syrup
2 teaspoons confectioners' sugar

1 Preheat oven to 350°F (325°F convection). Line baking sheet with parchment paper.

2 Cut four 4½-inch rounds from pastry; sprinkle with ground almonds. Top with figs; brush with combined butter and syrup. Turn edges of pastry up.

3 Bake galettes about 20 minutes or until pastry is puffed and golden. Serve warm, dusted with sifted confectioners' sugar.

prep + cook time 30 minutes **makes** 4

Apricot jam tart

2¼ cups all-purpose flour
½ cup confectioners' sugar
¾ cup (1½ sticks) cold butter, chopped
2 egg yolks
2 tablespoons iced water, approximately
⅔ cup apricot jam, warmed, sieved
1 tablespoon sliced almonds

apricot filling
2 cups coarsely chopped dried apricots
⅓ cup raisins
½ cup water
¼ cup sugar
2 tablespoons brandy
1 tablespoon fresh lemon zest

1 Process flour, sugar and butter until crumbly. With motor operating, add egg yolks and enough iced water to make ingredients cling together. Turn dough onto floured surface, knead gently until smooth. Shape dough into disc, enclose in plastic wrap; refrigerate 30 minutes.

2 Preheat oven to 325°F (300°F convection). Coat a 4½-inch x 13½-inch loose-based tart pan with cooking oil spray.

3 Meanwhile, make apricot filling.

4 Reserve one quarter of the dough. Roll remaining dough between sheets of parchment paper until large enough to line pan. Ease dough into pan, press into sides; trim edges, reserve excess dough. Spread apricot filling into pastry case; spread with jam.

5 Roll reserved dough between sheets of parchment paper until ¼-inch thick; using crinkle-cut pastry cutter, cut ½-inch strips from dough. Decorate tart in lattice pattern using pastry strips; sprinkle with nuts. Bake about 50 minutes.

apricot filling Cook ingredients, stirring, in medium saucepan, over medium heat about 10 minutes or until apricots soften. Cool 10 minutes. Blend or process apricot mixture until almost smooth.

prep + cook time 1 hour 40 minutes (+ refrigeration) **serves** 10

Hazelnut and date tart

1   sheet prepared pie dough
8   tablespoons (1 stick) butter, softened
⅓   cup sugar
2   tablespoons fresh lemon zest
2   eggs
1   cup ground hazelnuts
1   tablespoon all-purpose flour
1   teaspoon ground cinnamon
½   cup pitted dried dates, halved lengthways
½   cup honey, warmed

sesame cream
1¼   cups heavy cream
2   tablespoons sugar
2   teaspoons black sesame seeds
1   teaspoon vanilla extract
1   teaspoon sesame oil

1 Preheat oven to 400°F (375°F convection).

2 Line greased 10-inch round tart pan with pastry; press into base and sides, trim edge. Refrigerate 30 minutes.

3 Meanwhile, beat butter, sugar and zest in small bowl with electric mixer until combined. Beat in eggs, one at a time. Stir in ground hazelnuts, flour and cinnamon. Spread hazelnut filling into pastry case; top with dates.

4 Bake tart about 35 minutes or until firm. Brush hot tart with half the honey. Cool in pan.

5 Meanwhile, make sesame cream.

6 Serve tart drizzled with remaining honey; top with sesame cream.

sesame cream Beat cream and sugar in small bowl with electric mixer until soft peaks form; fold in remaining ingredients.

prep + cook time 55 minutes (+ refrigeration & cooling) **serves** 8

tip You can use ground almonds instead of ground hazelnuts if you prefer. Black sesame seeds are available from specialty spice shops.

Olive oil cake

3 eggs
1 cup sugar
1 tablespoon fresh orange zest
2¼ cups self-rising flour
¼ cup orange juice
½ cup skim milk
1 cup extra virgin olive oil
½ cup orange juice, warmed, extra
¼ cup confectioners' sugar

1 Preheat oven to 400°F (375°F convection). Coat a 9-inch square cake pan with olive oil.

2 Beat eggs, sugar and zest in medium bowl with electric mixer until thick and creamy and sugar is dissolved. Stir in sifted flour, then combined juice, milk and oil, in three batches. Pour mixture into pan.

3 Bake cake about 45 minutes. Stand cake in pan 5 minutes; turn, top-side up, onto wire rack placed over tray.

4 Pour extra juice over hot cake; dust with sifted confectioners' sugar. Cool cake before serving.

prep + cook time 1 hour 10 minutes **serves** 10

tip Lemon zest and juice can be substituted for the orange.

Walnut cake

  9 eggs, separated
¾ cup sugar
⅓ cup brandy
¾ cup orange juice
  1 teaspoon vanilla extract
1½ cups finely chopped walnuts
1½ cups packaged breadcrumbs
  1 teaspoon ground cinnamon
¼ teaspoon each ground cloves and allspice
  1 teaspoon baking soda

syrup
  1 cup sugar
  2 cups water
  1 cinnamon stick
  1 strip orange zest

1 Preheat oven to 400°F (375°F convection). Coat a 9 x 13-inch baking dish with cooking oil spray; line with parchment paper, extending paper 2 inches over short sides.

2 Beat egg yolks and ½ cup of the sugar in small bowl with electric mixer until light and fluffy. Transfer mixture to large bowl; stir in brandy, juice and extract, then nuts, breadcrumbs and sifted spices and soda.

3 Beat egg whites in large bowl with electric mixer until soft peaks form. Gradually add remaining sugar, beating until sugar dissolves between additions; fold into walnut mixture, in two batches. Pour mixture into dish.

4 Bake cake about 40 minutes. Cool cake in dish.

5 Meanwhile, make syrup.

6 Pour hot syrup over cake.

syrup Stir ingredients in small saucepan over heat until sugar dissolves. Bring to a boil; boil, uncovered, without stirring, 10 minutes.

prep + cook time 1 hour 15 minutes (+ cooling) **makes** 18

Coconut syrup cake

8 tablespoons (1 stick) butter, softened
1 cup sugar
4 eggs
2 cups sweetened, flaked coconut
1 cup self-rising flour
2 tablespoons sweetened, flaked coconut, extra

lemon syrup
1 cup sugar
1 cup water
4 (2-inch) strips lemon zest

1 Preheat oven to 325°F (300°F convection). Coat an 8-inch round cake pan with cooking spray; line base and side with parchment paper.

2 Beat butter and sugar in small bowl with electric mixer until light and fluffy. Beat in eggs one at a time. Transfer mixture to large bowl; stir in coconut and sifted flour. Spread mixture into pan; sprinkle with extra coconut.

3 Bake cake about 50 minutes.

4 Meanwhile, make lemon syrup.

5 Pour hot lemon syrup over hot cake in pan. Cool.

lemon syrup Stir ingredients in small saucepan over heat until sugar dissolves; bring to a boil. Reduce heat; simmer, uncovered, without stirring, 5 minutes. Strain.

prep + cook time 1 hour 10 minutes (+ cooling) **serves** 12

Yogurt cake

8 tablespoons (1 stick) butter, softened
1 cup sugar
3 eggs, separated
2 cups self-rising flour
½ teaspoon baking soda
¼ cup finely chopped blanched almonds
1 cup yogurt

1 Preheat oven to 350°F (325°F convection). Coat a 9-inch x 13-inch baking pan with cooking oil spray; line base and sides with parchment paper.

2 Beat butter and sugar in small bowl with electric mixer until light and fluffy. Beat in egg yolks.

3 Transfer mixture to large bowl; stir in sifted flour and soda, in two batches. Stir in nuts and yogurt.

4 Beat egg whites in clean small bowl with electric mixer until soft peaks form. Fold egg whites into yogurt mixture, in two batches. Spread mixture into pan.

5 Bake cake about 35 minutes. Turn cake onto wire rack to cool.

prep + cook time 1 hour (+ cooling) **serves** 12
serving suggestion Dusted icing sugar.

Pistachio honey cake

¾ cup honey
⅔ cup sugar
1 tablespoon brandy
1 tablespoon lemon juice
½ cup olive oil
2 eggs
5 ounces ricotta cheese
2 cups self-rising flour
½ teaspoon each of ground cinnamon, nutmeg and clove
¼ cup shelled unsalted pistachio nuts
1 tablespoon honey, extra

1 Stir honey, sugar, brandy and juice in small saucepan over heat until sugar dissolves; bring to a boil. Reduce heat, simmer, uncovered, 2 minutes. Cool 20 minutes.

2 Meanwhile, preheat oven to 300°F (275°F convection). Coat a 5½-inch x 8½-inch loaf pan with cooking oil spray; line base and two long sides with parchment paper.

3 Combine oil, eggs and cheese in large bowl; stir in sifted dry ingredients and cooled honey mixture. Spread mixture into pan; sprinkle with nuts.

4 Bake cake about 1 hour. Turn cake, top-side up, onto wire rack. Drizzle with extra honey; cool before cutting.

prep + cook time 1 hour 30 minutes (+ cooling) **serves** 10

Moist carrot and apple cake

2 cups self-rising flour
1 teaspoon baking soda
1 cup sugar
4 cups coarsely grated carrot
2 cups coarsely grated apple
1 tablespoon fresh orange zest
¼ cup orange juice
¾ cup olive oil
⅓ cup brandy
1 cup toasted pine nuts
2 teaspoons confectioners' sugar

1 Preheat oven to 350°F (325°F convection). Coat a 10-inch springform pan with cooking oil spray; line base and side with parchment paper.

2 Sift flour and soda into large bowl; stir in sugar, carrot, apple and zest. Stir in juice, oil, brandy and pine nuts. Pour mixture into pan.

3 Bake cake about 1 hour. Stand cake 10 minutes before removing from springform pan. Serve dusted with sifted icing sugar.

prep + cook time 1 hour 20 minutes (+ standing) **serves** 12

Chocolate and orange polenta cake

1 cup sugar
1½ cups water
2 small oranges, sliced
¼ cup water, extra
8 tablespoons (1 stick) butter, softened
1 tablespoon fresh orange zest
1 cup firmly packed light brown sugar
3 eggs
½ cup all-purpose flour

½ cup self-rising flour
½ teaspoon baking soda
½ cup cocoa powder
½ cup ground almonds
½ cup polenta
⅓ cup sour cream
¼ cup orange juice
3 ounces semi-sweet chocolate, finely chopped

1 Preheat oven to 350°F (325°F convection). Grease deep 8-inch round cake pan; line base and side with two layers of parchment paper.

2 Stir sugar and the water in large skillet over medium heat, without boiling, until sugar dissolves. Bring to a boil. Reduce heat; simmer, uncovered, without stirring, 5 minutes or until syrup thickens slightly. Add orange slices; simmer gently, uncovered, about 7 minutes or until rind is tender, turning slices halfway through cooking time.

3 Remove from heat; using tongs, lift orange slices from syrup and place in base of pan, slightly overlapping each slice. Reserve syrup.

4 Add the extra water to reserved syrup in pan; bring to the boil. Reduce heat; simmer, uncovered, without stirring, until syrup is a light honey color. Pour two-thirds of hot syrup over orange slices; reserve remaining syrup.

5 Beat butter, zest and brown sugar in small bowl with electric mixer until light and fluffy. Beat in eggs, one at a time. Transfer to large bowl; stir in sifted flours, soda and cocoa, then ground almonds, polenta, sour cream, juice and chocolate. Carefully spread mixture over oranges in pan.

6 Bake cake about 1¼ hours. Stand cake in pan 15 minutes; turn onto serving plate. Spoon reserved syrup over oranges.

prep + cook time 2 hours **serves** 8

serving suggestion Ice cream or cream.

Date nut balls

10 fresh dates, pitted, coarsely chopped
½ cup raisins
½ cup coarsely chopped toasted walnuts
1½ tablespoons sweet red wine
7 ounces semi-sweet chocolate chips
(70% cocoa solids), melted
⅓ cup finely chopped toasted walnuts

1 Blend or process dates, raisins, coarsely chopped nuts and wine until mixture forms a smooth paste.

2 Using wet hands, roll level teaspoons of mixture into balls; place on baking sheets lined with parchment paper. Cover; refrigerate overnight.

3 Dip half the balls in melted chocolate, place on foil-lined tray; leave to set at room temperature. Roll remaining balls in finely chopped nuts.

prep time 30 minutes (+ refrigeration) **makes** 50

tip You can use orange juice in place of the sweet red wine if desired.

Almond turron

2 sheets confectioners' rice paper
3 cups blanched almonds, roasted
½ cup honey
1⅓ cups sugar
2 tablespoons water
1 egg white

1 Grease 3-inch x 10½-inch bar cake pan. Line base and long sides with parchment paper, extending paper 2 inches over long sides. Place one sheet of rice paper in pan, covering base and up long sides.

2 Stir honey, sugar and the water in small saucepan over low heat until sugar dissolves. Using pastry brush dipped in water, brush down side of pan to dissolve all sugar crystals. Bring syrup to a boil; boil, uncovered, without stirring, about 10 minutes or until syrup reaches 327°F on candy thermometer. Remove from heat.

3 Just before syrup is ready, beat egg white in small heatproof bowl with electric mixer until soft peaks form. With motor operating, add hot syrup to egg white in a thin, steady stream. Beat until all syrup is added and mixture thickens.

4 Working quickly, transfer egg white mixture to large bowl; stir in nuts. Spoon mixture into pan; press firmly. Trim remaining sheet of rice paper to fit top of nougat; press on lightly, smoothing surface. Stand 2 hours or until cooled to room temperature and firm, before cutting.

prep + cook time 35 minutes (+ standing) **makes** 25

tip A candy thermometer, available from kitchenware stores, is essential for this recipe. Place thermometer in large saucepan of simmering water while syrup is heating. This will stop thermometer cracking when placed in hot syrup. Once syrup is at correct temperature, return thermometer to pan of water; remove from heat. When cool, rinse and dry. You will need a powerful electric mixer. Standing mixers generally have more powerful motors than most hand-held electric mixers. Rice paper is edible and ready to use. It can be bought from specialty food stores; don't confuse this paper with the rice paper used in "rice paper rolls" which needs soaking to soften. Use a lightly oiled knife to cut turron. Turron can be made a week ahead; store in airtight container in a cool, dry place. Do not refrigerate.

Mint tea

5 cups boiling water
1 cup firmly packed fresh mint
¼ cup sugar
½ ounce green tea leaves

1 Combine 1 cup of the water and ⅔ cup of the mint in medium glass measuring cup; drain, reserve mint.

2 Stir drained mint, the remaining water, sugar and tea in medium saucepan over heat until sugar dissolves. Bring to a boil.

3 Strain tea into large heatproof teapot.

4 Serve cups of tea topped with remaining mint.

prep + cook time 15 minutes **makes** 5 cups

Hot chocolate

4 cups milk
2-inch strips orange zest
1 cinnamon stick
6 ounces semi-sweet chocolate, finely chopped

1 Bring milk, zest and cinnamon to a boil in medium saucepan. Remove from heat; stand, covered, 5 minutes.

2 Discard zest and cinnamon. Add chocolate; stir until smooth.

prep + cook time 15 minutes (+ standing) **serves** 6

349

Spiced coffee with rosewater cream

8 cardamom pods
3 cinnamon sticks
4 cloves
¾ cup instant coffee granules
4 cups water
¼ cup light brown sugar
⅓ cup cream
1 teaspoon rosewater

1 Toast spices in small dry skillet until fragrant.

2 Combine spices, coffee, the water and sugar in medium saucepan; stir over heat until sugar dissolves. Bring to a boil. Reduce heat; simmer, stirring occasionally, 10 minutes.

3 Meanwhile, beat cream and rosewater in small bowl with electric mixer until soft peaks form.

4 Strain hot coffee into serving cups; serve topped with rosewater cream.

prep + cook time 15 minutes **makes** 4 cups

Greek coffee

1 cup cold water
1½ tablespoons ground Greek coffee
3 teaspoons sugar

1 Place the water in 4 demitasse-cup capacity briki or small saucepan. Add coffee and sugar; stir over low heat until sugar dissolves. Slowly bring to a boil; remove from heat when froth almost reaches the top of briki.

2 Divide froth among 4 demitasse cups, then carefully fill the cups with remaining coffee mixture.

3 Serve coffee immediately with a glass of cold water.

prep + cook time 10 minutes **serves** 4

tip A traditional briki (small pot) is the best pot to use when making Greek coffee because it allows the proper amount of froth to form which in turn adds to the unique taste. Brikis are available from Greek and Middle Eastern grocery stores. A demitasse cup holds about ¼ cup.

glossary

allspice
also called pimento or jamaican pepper; tastes like a combination of nutmeg, cumin, cinnamon and clove. It is available whole or ground from most supermarkets and specialty food stores.

almonds

blanched
almonds with brown skins removed.

flaked
paper-thin slices.

ground
also known as almond meal.

slivered
small pieces cut lengthways.

artichoke hearts tender center of the globe artichoke; is harvested from the plant after the prickly choke is removed. Cooked hearts can be bought from delis or canned in brine.

arugula
also called rugula and rucola; peppery green leaf eaten raw in salads or used in cooking. Baby rocket leaves are smaller and less peppery.

baking paper
also called parchment paper or baking parchment; a silicone-coated paper primarily used for lining baking pans and oven trays so cakes and biscuits won't stick.

bay leaves
aromatic leaves from the bay tree available fresh or dried; adds a strong, slightly peppery flavor.

beans

broad (fava)
available dried, fresh, canned and frozen. Peel fresh beans twice—the outer green pod and beige-green inner shell.

lima
large, flat kidney-shaped, beige dried and canned beans. Also known as butter beans.

blood orange
a virtually seedless citrus fruit with blood-red-streaked zest and flesh; sweet, non-acidic, salmon-colored pulp and juice with slight strawberry or raspberry overtones. The zest is not as bitter as an ordinary orange.

breadcrumbs

fresh
bread, usually white, processed into crumbs.

packaged
prepared fine-textured, crunchy white bread-crumbs; good for coating foods that are to be fried.

stale
crumbs made by grating, blending or processing 1- or 2-day-old bread.

butter
we use salted butter; 1 stick is equal to 4 ounces.

buttermilk
originally the term given to the slightly sour liquid left after butter was churned from cream, today it is commercially made similarly to yogurt. Sold alongside fresh milk products in supermarkets. Despite the implication of its name, it is low in fat.

capers
the grey-green buds of a Mediterranean shrub, sold either dried and salted or pickled in a vinegar brine.

cardamom
a spice native to India; can be purchased in pod, seed or ground form. Has a distinctive, aromatic, sweetly rich flavor.

cayenne pepper
a thin-fleshed, long, extremely hot dried red chilli, usually purchased ground.

cheese

bocconcini
from the diminutive of "boccone," meaning mouthful in Italian; walnut-sized, baby mozzarella, a delicate, semi-soft, white cheese. Sold fresh, it spoils rapidly; refrigerate in brine for 1 or 2 days.

feta
see essentials, page 9

goat
made from goat's milk; has an earthy, strong taste. Available soft, crumbly and firm, in various shapes and sizes, and sometimes rolled in ash or herbs.

parmesan
also called parmigiano; is a hard, grainy cow's-milk cheese originating in the Parma region of Italy.

ricotta
a soft, sweet, moist, white cow-milk cheese with a low fat content and a slightly grainy

texture. Its name roughly translates as "cooked again" and refers to ricotta's manufacture from a whey that is itself a by-product of other cheese making.

chicken

breast fillet
breast halved, skinned, boned.

drumettes
small fleshy part of the wing between shoulder and elbow, trimmed to resemble a drumstick.

drumsticks
leg with skin and bone intact.

small chicken
also called spatchcock or poussin; no more than 6 weeks old, weighing a maximum of 1 pound. Spatchcock is also a cooking term to describe splitting poultry open, flattening and grilling.

tenderloins
thin strip of meat lying just under the breast.

thigh cutlets
thigh with skin and center bone intact; sometimes found skinned with bone intact.

thigh fillets
thigh with skin and center bone removed.

chickpeas
also known as garbanzo beans; an irregularly round, sandy-colored legume. It has a firm texture even after cooking, a floury mouth-feel and robust nutty flavor; available canned or dried (reconstitute for several hours in cold water before use).

chili
use rubber gloves when seeding and chopping fresh chilies as they can burn your skin. We use unseeded chilies because the seeds contain the heat; use fewer chilies rather than seeding the lot.

chocolate, semi-sweet
made of a high percentage of cocoa liquor and cocoa butter, and little added sugar. Unless stated otherwise, we use dark chocolate as it's ideal for use in desserts and cakes.

cinnamon
available in pieces (sticks or quills) and ground into powder; one of the world's most common spices, used as a sweet, fragrant flavoring for sweet and savory dishes.

cloves
dried flower buds of a tropical tree; can be used whole or in ground form. They have a strong scent and taste so should be used sparingly.

cumin
also called zeera or comino; the dried seed of a plant related to the parsley family. It has a spicy, almost curry-like flavor and is available dried as seeds or ground.

dill
used fresh or dried, as seeds or ground, it adds an anise, celery sweetness to foods. Its feathery, frond-like fresh leaves are grassier and more subtle than the dried version or the seeds.

dried currants
tiny, almost black raisins so-named after a grape variety that originated in Corinth, Greece. These are not the same as fresh currants, which are the fruit of a plant in the gooseberry family.

eggs
if a recipe calls for raw or barely cooked eggs, exercise caution if there is a salmonella problem in your area, particularly in food eaten by children and pregnant women.

fennel
also called finocchio or anise; a crunchy green vegetable slightly resembling celery. Is eaten raw, fried or used as an ingredient in soups and sauces. Also the name given to the dried seeds of the plant which have a stronger licorice flavor.

figs
originally from the countries that border the eastern Mediterranean; are best eaten in peak season, at the height of summer. Vary in skin and flesh color according to type not ripeness. When ripe, figs should be unblemished and bursting with flesh; nectar beads at the base indicate when a fig is at its best.

harissa
a North African paste made from dried red chilies, garlic, olive oil and caraway seeds; can be used as a rub for meat, an ingredient in sauces and dressings, or eaten as a condiment. The paste (in a tube) is very hot and should

not be used in large amounts; bottled harissa sauce is more mild. It is available from Middle Eastern food shops and some supermarkets.

lamb shanks forequarter leg; sometimes sold as frenched shanks if the gristle and narrow end of the bone are discarded and the remaining meat trimmed.

lemon thyme
an herb with a lemony scent, which is due to the high level of citral in its leaves—an oil also found in lemon, orange, verbena and lemon grass. The citrus scent is enhanced by crushing the leaves in your hands before using the herb.

lentils
(red, brown, yellow) dried pulses often identified by and named after their color. Eaten by cultures all over the world, most famously perhaps in the dhals of India, lentils have high food value.

marjoram
closely related to and similar in flavor to oregano, but milder and sweeter. A delicious addition to herb mixtures. As with oregano, many chefs prefer dried marjoram to fresh.

mesclun
pronounced mess-kluhn; also called mixed greens or spring salad mix. A commercial blend of assorted young lettuce and other green leaves, including baby spinach leaves, mizuna and curly endive.

milk
we use whole milk unless stated otherwise.

mushrooms
button
small, cultivated white mushrooms with a mild flavor.

portobello
are mature, fully opened swiss browns; they are larger and bigger in flavor.

swiss brown
also called roman or cremini. Light to dark brown in color with full-bodied flavor.

nutmeg
a strong and pungent spice. Usually purchased ground, the flavor is more intense freshly grated from the whole nut (available from spice shops).

oil
avocado
is pressed from the flesh of the avocado fruit. Has a high smoking point. It is high in monounsaturated fats and vitamin E.

cooking-spray
we use a cholesterol-free spray made from canola oil.

olive
made from ripened olives. Extra virgin and virgin are the first and second press, respectively, of the olives and are therefore considered the best.

vegetable
from plant rather than animal fats.

onion
red
also called spanish, red spanish or bermuda onion; a sweet-flavored, large, purple-red onion.

scallion
also called, incorrectly, shallot; an immature onion picked before the bulb has formed, has a long, bright-green edible stalk.

spring
crisp, narrow green-leafed tops and a round sweet white bulb larger than scallions.

oregano
an herb, also called wild marjoram; has a woody stalk and clumps of tiny, dark-green leaves. Has a pungent, peppery flavor.

orzo
a small rice-sized pasta. It can be replaced by risoni which is slightly smaller.

ouzo
an anise-flavored Greek spirit.

pancetta
an Italian unsmoked bacon. Used sliced or chopped as an ingredient, rather than eaten on its own.

paprika
ground dried sweet red bell pepper; also available sweet, hot, mild and smoked.

pine nuts
also known as pignoli; not a nut but a small, cream-colored kernel from pine cones. They are best toasted in a dry skillet until fragrant before use to bring out the flavor.

pita bread
also called lebanese bread. A wheat-flour pocket bread sold in large, flat pieces that separate into rounds. Also available in small pieces called pocket pita.

polenta
also called cornmeal; a flour-like cereal made of dried corn. Also the dish made from it.

preserved lemon rind
lemons preserved in salt and lemon juice or water. Sold in jars at delis and some supermarkets; once opened, keep refrigerated. To use, remove and discard pulp, squeeze juice from rind; slice rind thinly. Use the rind only and rinse well under cold water before using.

prosciutto
a kind of unsmoked Italian ham; salted, air-cured and aged, it is usually eaten uncooked.

quail
a small, delicate-flavored farmed game bird related to the pheasant and partridge; usually weighs about ½ pound.

radicchio
a red-leafed Italian chicory with a refreshing bitter taste; eaten raw and cooked.

rice

arborio
small, round grain rice well-suited to absorb a large amount of liquid; the high level of starch makes it suitable for risottos.

basmati
a white, fragrant long-grained rice; the grains fluff up when cooked. It should be washed several times before cooking.

wild
not a member of the rice family but the seed of an aquatic grass native to North America. Wild rice has a strong nutty taste and can be expensive, so is best combined with brown and white rices.

risoni
small rice-shape pasta; similar to another small pasta, orzo.

roasting/toasting spread nuts and dried coconut evenly on oven tray; roast in moderate oven about 5 minutes. Stir desiccated coconut, pine nuts and sesame seeds over low heat in heavy-based skillet until fragrant.

rosewater
extract made from crushed rose petals, called gulab in India; used for its aromatic quality in many sweet-meats and desserts.

saffron
the stigma of a member of the crocus family, available ground or in strands; imparts a yellow-orange color to food once infused. The quality can vary greatly; the best is the world's most expensive spice.

seafood

mussels
should only be bought from a reliable fish market: they must be tightly closed when bought, indicating they are alive. Before cooking, scrub shells with a strong brush and remove the beards; do not eat any that do not open after cooking. Varieties include black and green-lip.

shrimp
can be purchased cooked or uncooked, with or without shells.

squid
also called calamari; a type of mollusk. Buy squid hoods to make preparation and cooking faster.

white fish fillets
means fillets from non-oily fish; includes cod, whiting, flounder, and snapper

semolina
coarsely ground flour milled from durum wheat; the flour used in making gnocchi, pasta and couscous.

sesame seeds
black and white are the most common of this small oval seed. The seeds are used as an ingredient and as a condiment. Roast in a heavy-based skillet over low heat.

shallots
also called french shallots, golden shallots or eschalots. Small and elongated, with a brown-skin, they grow in tight clusters similar to garlic.

sour cream
a thick, commercially-cultured sour cream with a minimum fat content of 35 percent.

spinach
also called English spinach and, incorrectly, silver beet.

split peas
yellow or green varieties, both with a sweet, strong pea flavor. They are usually pre-soaked but may be cooked without soaking.

star anise
a dried star-shaped pod whose seeds have an astringent aniseed flavor; used to flavor stocks and marinades.

sugar

brown
a soft, finely granulated sugar retaining molasses for its color and flavor.

sweet potato
the orange-fleshed sweet potato is often confused with yam; good baked, boiled, mashed or fried similarly to other potatoes.

Swiss chard
also called, incorrectly, spinach; has fleshy stalks and large leaves, both of which can be prepared as for spinach.

tahini
see essentials, page 8

tomato

bottled pasta sauce
a prepared sauce; a blend of tomatoes, herbs and spices.

paste
triple-concentrated tomato puree used to flavor soups, stews and sauces.

puree
canned pureed tomatoes (not tomato paste).

roma
these are smallish, oval-shaped tomatoes much used in Italian cooking or salads.

sun-dried
tomato pieces that have been dried with salt; this dehydrates the tomato and concentrates the flavor. We use sun-dried tomatoes packaged in oil, unless otherwise specified.

truss
small vine-ripened tomatoes with vine still attached.

vanilla

bean
dried, long, thin pod; the minuscule black seeds inside are used to impart a vanilla flavor in baking and desserts.

extract
obtained from vanilla beans infused in water; a non-alcoholic version of essence.

vinegar

balsamic
originally from Modena, Italy, there are now many balsamic vinegars on the market ranging in pungency and quality. Quality can be determined up to a point by price; use the most expensive sparingly.

cider
made from fermented apples.

watercress
one of the cress family, a large group of peppery greens used raw in salads, dips and sandwiches, or cooked in soups. Highly perishable, so it must be used as soon as possible after purchase.

yogurt
we use plain yogurt unless otherwise specified.

zucchini
small, pale- or dark-green or yellow vegetable belonging to the squash family.

index

A

Aioli, 170
  Green onion, 190
Almond(s), *see* Nut(s)
Anchovies
  Cauliflower with garlic, chilies
    and, 118
  Fish parcels with, and olives, 162
  Kalamata olive dressing, 153
  Olive and cheese fritters, 19
Apple
  cake, Moist carrot and, 338
Apricot(s)
  jam tart, filling, 325
  Stuffed peppers, 289
Artichoke(s)
  Fava beans and, 270
  in oregano vinaigrette, 109
  pizzetta, Feta and, 47
  spinach dip, 35
Arugula
  Honeyed orange quails, 229
Asparagus
  Grilled
    lemon thyme chicken, 226
    salmon with chermoulla sauce, 173
Avgolemono
  about: soup tip, 82
Avocado(s)
  Honey lemon dressing, 90
  Valencian salad, 93

B

Bacon
  Seafood soup, 78
Baked
  cabbage with tomatoes, 114
  fish with saffron, leek and potato,
    161
  lamb shanks with orzo, 255
Baklava, 321
Basil
  Braised borlotti beans with tomato
    and garlic, 269
  Chicken in red wine and tomato
    sauce, 225
  Green olive butter, 202
  Grilled salmon with pepper and olive
    salsa, 174
  Lamb kefta, 248
  Lemon and herb fish with chickpea
    salad, 150
  Pan-fried fish with fennel and olive
    salad, 146

Scallop and fish skewers with tomato
    salad, 141
  Soft shell crabs with green onion aioli,
    190
  Tomato dressing, 270
Bay leaves
  Greek chicken and vegetable soup, 81
  Slow-cooked potatoes with wine
    and herbs, 122
  Spicy chicken and rice, 213
  Tomato dressing, 270
  Vegetable kebab, 282
  Winter soup with oxtail and chickpeas,
    86
Bean(s)
  Borlotti
    Braised, with tomato and garlic, 269
  Cannellini
    Crisp fish with paprika mustard
      butter, 154
  Fava
    and artichokes, 270
    patties with minted yogurt, 23
    Tuna with lentils and, 166
  Green
    Braised, 273
    Eggplant, tomato and chickpea
      casserole, 266
    Fish tagine, 177
    with tomato walnut sauce, 113
  White
    dip with pita crisps, 39
Beef
  Ground
    and fig cigars, 56
    kefta with green onion couscous,
      239
    Meatballs in tomato sauce, 60
    Spiced meatballs with romesco sauce,
      59
  Skirt steak
    soup, Shredded, 85
  Stock
    kefta with green onion couscous,
      239
    Lamb kefta, 248
    Pastitsio, 243
    Veal, quince and caramelized onion
      tagine, 244
    Winter soup with oxtail and
      chickpeas, 86
  Tenderloin(s)
    kebabs with roasted vegetable
      salad, 236

Bell pepper(s)
  about: chili family, varieties, 10
  Beef kebabs with roasted
    vegetable salad, 236
  brown rice, Olive and, 134
  Cheese and tomato tortilla, 290
  Chicken and chorizo salad with
    garlic mayonnaise, 205
  with lentil salsa, 198
  Chorizo cones with salsa, 63
  Goat cheese with chickpeas and, 40
  Green beans with tomato walnut
    sauce, 113
  Grilled seafood with aioli, 170
  Lemon and herb fish with chickpea
    salad, 150
  Olive salsa, 174
  Pan-fried fish with fennel and olive
    salad, 146
  Radish and herb salad, 106
  salad, Roasted, 138
  Shredded beef soup, 85
  Spanish rice, 217
  Spicy chicken and rice, 213
  Stuffed, 289
  Vegetable paella, 286
  White beans and lentils, 281
Beet(s)
  salad, 97
  Vegetable kebabs, 282
Braised
  borlotti beans with tomato and garlic,
    269
  chicken with chickpeas, lemon and
    garlic, 222
  green beans, 273
Bread(s)
  French
    Lemon feta toast, 73
    Tomato and feta toasts, 32
  Pita
    crisps, White bean dip with, 39
    Grilled chicken with tomato salad,
      201
    Lamb kebabs with yogurt and, 247
    Radish and herb salad, 106
  White
    Skordalia, 142
Breadcrumbs
  Almond sauce, 206
  Chickpea patties with tahini sauce,
    20
  Fava bean patties with minted yogurt,
    23

Lamb
    kefta, 248
    meatballs with egg-lemon sauce,
        252
    Meatballs in tomato sauce, 60
    Paella croquettes, 24
    Spiced meatballs with romesco
        sauce, 59
    Walnut cake, 330

C

Cabbage
    Baked, with tomatoes, 114
Calamari
    Deep-fried, 51
Cantaloupe
    Melon salad with citrus sugar, 298
Caper(s)
    and parsley topping, 48
Carrot(s)
    and apple cake, Moist, 338
    and olive salad, 260
    and sweet potatoes, Honey-spiced,
        126
    raisin and herb salad, 105
    Shredded beef soup, 85
    Slow-roasted spiced lamb shoulder,
        259
    Sweet and spicy vegetable tagine, 278
    Tuna with lentils and beans, 166
Cauliflower
    couscous, Spiced, 117
    with garlic, chilies and anchovies, 118
Cheese(s)
    Bocconcini fritters, Olive and, 19
    Cheddar
        Chorizo and potato tortilla, 125
    Cottage cheese
        phyllo triangles, 44
    Cream cheese
        Sardine dip, 28
    Feta
        about: sheep and cow varieties, 9
        and artichoke pizzetta, 47
        and pine nut salad, Spinach, 94
        and tomato tortilla, 290
        Chicken phyllo pie, 233
        phyllo triangles, 44
        Saganaki shrimp, 52
        Slow-cooked potatoes with wine
            and herbs, 122
        toast, Lemon, 73
        toasts, Tomato and, 32
    Goat
        with chickpeas and bell peppers, 40
    Haloumi
        about: Greek cooking, 9

Kasseri
    Chickpea patties with tahini sauce,
        20
Manchego
    about: Spanish, 9
    Valencian salad, 93
Mozzarella
    Chorizo and potato tortilla, 125
Parmesan
    Lamb meatballs with egg-lemon
        sauce, 252
Pecorino romano
    Artichoke spinach dip, 35
    Meatballs in tomato sauce, 60
    Moussaka, 240
    Pastitsio, 243
    Stuffed eggplant with lamb and
        rice, 251
Ricotta
    Pistachio honey cake, 337
sauce, 243
Chermoulla, 169
    chicken with onion couscous, 209
    dressing, 110
    Roasted white fish with, 169
    sauce, 173
    shrimp skewers, 186
Cherry spoon sweet, 301
Chicken
    Breast(s)
        and chorizo salad with garlic
            mayonnaise, 205
        Chermoulla, with onion couscous,
            209
        Grilled
            with green olive butter, 202
            with tomato salad, 201
        lemon and rice soup, 82
        with almond sauce, 206
        with olives and couscous, 210
        phyllo pie, 233
    Cornish hens
        Lemon thyme and chili roast, 230
    Drumettes
        Spicy chicken and rice, 213
    Drumsticks
        tagine with figs and walnuts, 221
    Legs
        Grilled lemon thyme, 226
        tagine with dried plums, 218
    Smoked
        Paella croquettes, 24
    Stock
        Almond sauce, 206
        Baked fish with saffron, leek and
            potato, 161
        Baked lamb shank with orzo, 255

Braised, with chickpeas, lemon
    and garlic, 222
Chickpea, garlic and mint soup, 74
Cream
    of roasted garlic and potato soup,
        70
    of spinach soup, with lemon feta
        toast, 73
Grilled lemon thyme chicken, 226
Honeyed lamb shanks, 256
in red wine and tomato sauce, 225
Lamb meatballs with egg-lemon
    sauce, 252
Lemon and herb fish with
    chickpea salad, 150
    and rice soup, 82
Lentil soup, 66
Onion couscous, 209
Paella croquettes, 24
phyllo pie, 233
Saffron cinnamon couscous, 130
Slow-cooked potatoes with wine
    and herbs, 122
Spicy chicken and rice, 213
Spicy couscous, 128
tagine
    with dried plums, 218
    with figs and walnuts, 221
Tuna with lentils and beans, 166
Turnip soup, 69
with olives and couscous, 210
Tenderloin(s) with lentil salsa, 198
Thigh(s)
    Braised, with chickpeas, lemon and
        garlic, 222
    Grilled, with Spanish rice, 217
    in red wine and tomato sauce, 225
    kebabs with harissa mayonnaise,
        214
    phyllo pie, 233
    souvlaki, Mini, 55
    tagine with figs and walnuts, 221
Whole
    and vegetable soup, Greek, 81
Chickpea(s)
    about: uses, textures, flavor, 10
    Braised chicken with, lemons and
        garlic, 222
    garlic and mint soup, 74
    Goat cheese with, and bell peppers,
        40
    Moroccan-style vegetables, 285
    Onion couscous, 209
    patties with tahini sauce, 20
    salad, Lemon and herb fish with,
        150
    tomato stew, 77

Vegetable tagine, 274
Winter soup with oxtail and, 86
Chili(es)
  Red
    Braised
      chicken with chickpeas, lemon
        and garlic, 222
      green beans, 273
    Cauliflower with garlic, and
      anchovies, 118
    Chermoulla, 169
    Garlic shrimp, 189
    marinade Lemon thyme and, 230
    Mussels with tomatoes and, 193
    Olive and bell peppers brown rice,
      134
    Shredded beef soup, 85
    Shrimp and zucchini with mint pilaf,
      131
  Red Thai
    Chicken with lentil salsa, 198
    tomato salsa, 63
    Grilled chicken with Spanish rice,
      217
    Lamb kefta, 248
    Moroccan-style vegetables, 285
    Saffron cinnamon couscous, 130
Chive(s)
  Beef and fig cigars, 56
Chorizo
  about: pork and beef, uses, 11
  and potato tortilla, 125
  Chicken and, salad with garlic
    mayonnaise, 205
  cones with salsa, 63
  Crisp fish with paprika mustard butter,
    154
  Paella croquettes, 24
  Spiced meatballs with romesco sauce,
    59
  Winter soup with oxtail and
    chickpeas, 86
Cilantro
  Beef
    kebabs with roasted vegetable
      salad, 236
    kefta with green onion couscous,
      239
  Carrot and olive salad, 260
  Chicken
    with lentil salsa, 198
    with olives and couscous, 210
  Chermoulla, 209
    shrimp skewers, 186
  Chili tomato salsa, 63
  Clams with white wine and tomatoes,
    194

couscous, Saffron, 130
dressing, Shrimp and couscous salad
  with lemon, 182
Eggplant dip, 36
Green beans with tomato walnut
  sauce, 113
Grilled chicken with Spanish rice, 217
Lamb kefta, 248
Radish and herb salad, 106
Spiced cauliflower couscous, 117
Cinnamon
  Baked lamb shanks with orzo, 255
  Baklava, 321
  Chicken
    tagine with figs and walnuts, 221
    with olives and couscous, 210
  couscous, Saffron, 130
  Figs in orange syrup with yogurt
    cream, 302
  flan, 310
  Hazelnut and date tart, 326
  Honeyed lamb shanks, 256
  Hot chocolate, 349
  Lamb kebabs with yogurt and pita
    bread, 247
  Loukoumades, 314
  Moussaka, 240
  Moroccan-style vegetables, 285
  Pastitsio, 243
  Rice pudding with, and vanilla, 305
  Saffron panna cotta with honeyed
    figs, 306
  Spiced
    coffee with rosewater cream, 350
    oranges with brown sugar toffee,
      294
  Veal, quince and caramelized onion
    tagine, 244
  Walnut cake syrup, 330
Citrus sugar, 298
Clams with white wine and tomatoes, 194
Clove(s)
  Baklava, 321
  Cinnamon flan, 310
  Spiced coffee with rosemary cream,
    350
  Spiced syrup, 318
  Walnut cake, 330
Coconut syrup cake, 333
Coffee
  Greek, 353
  Spiced, with rosewater cream, 350
Corn
  Shredded beef soup, 85
  Spanish rice, 217
  Spicy chicken and rice, 213
Cottage cheese, see Cheese(s)

Couscous
  about: origins, uses, 13
  Chicken with olives and, 210
  green onion, Beef kefta with, 239
  Lemon, 274
  Lemon pistachio, 149
  Onion, 209
  Saffron cinnamon, 130
  salad with lemon cilantro dressing,
    Shrimp and, 182
  Spiced cauliflower, 117
  Spicy, 129
Crab(s)
  Soft shell, with green onion aioli,
    190
Cream
  of roasted garlic and potato soup,
    70
  of spinach soup with lemon feta toast,
    73
Crème caramel, Spiced, 309
Crisp fish with paprika mustard butter,
  154
Cucumber(s)
  and orange salad, Sweet, 90
  Chicken with lentil salsa,198
  Tomato salad, 201
Currant(s)
  Spicy couscous, 128

D
Date(s)
  Fresh peaches and, with orange
    blossom water, 297
  nut balls, 342
  tart, Hazelnut and, 326
Deep-fried
  baby calamari, 51
  eggplant with fresh herb sauce, 27
Dill
  Beet salad, 97
  Chicken phyllo pie, 233
  Dolmades, 43
  Lamb meatballs with egg-lemon
    sauce, 252
  Lentil soup, 66
  Pickled zucchini salad, 89
  Spinach, feta and pine nut salad, 94
Dolmades, 43
Dukkah
  about: seed, nut and spice mix, 214
  Vegetable kebab dressing, 282

E
Egg(s)
  Almond turron, 345
  Apricot jam tart, 325

Beef kefta with green onion couscous, 239
Cheese
    and tomato tortilla, 290
    phyllo triangles, 44
Chickpea patties with tahini sauce, 20
Chicken
    lemon and rice soup, 82
    phyllo pie, 233
Chocolate and orange polenta cake, 341
Chorizo and potato tortilla, 125
Cinnamon flan, 310
Coconut syrup cake, 333
Fava bean patties with minted yogurt, 23
Galaktoboureko, 313
Honey walnut cookies, 318
Lamb
    kebabs with yogurt and pita bread, 247
    kefta, 248
    meatballs with egg-lemon sauce, 252
Meatballs in tomato sauce, 60
Olive oil cake, 329
Paella croquettes, 24
Pastitsio, 243
Pistachio honey cake, 337
Rice pudding with cinnamon and vanilla, 305
Salt-baked whole snapper with fennel and mint salad, 158
Spiced crème caramel, 309
Walnut cake, 330
Yogurt cake, 334
Eggplant(s)
    Deep-fried, with fresh herb sauce, 27
    dip, 36
    Moroccan-style vegetables, 285
    Moussaka, 240
    Roasted, with marjoram vinaigrette, 102
    salad, 101
    Stuffed, with lamb and rice, 251
    tomato and chickpea casserole, 266

F

Fava bean(s), see Bean(s)
Fennel
    and mint salad, Salt-baked whole snapper with, 158
    and olive salad, Pan-fried fish with, 146
    braised, Oven-roasted fish with 165
    Fish tagine, 177
    sauce, Tomato and, 185
    Seafood soup, 78

Slow-roasted spiced lamb shoulder, 259
Feta, see Cheese(s)
Fig(s)
    Beef and, cigars, 56
    Chicken tagine with, and walnuts, 221
    galettes, 322
    Honeyed, 306
    in orange syrup with yogurt cream, 302
Fish
    Salmon
        Grilled, with chermoulla sauce, 173
        Salt Cod and potato pie, 178
    Sardine(s)
        dip, 28
        with caper and parsley topping, 48
    sauce
        Lemon cilantro dressing, 182
    Snapper
        Roasted, with chermoulla, 169
        Salt-baked whole, with fennel and mint salad, 158
    stock
        Oven-roasted fish with braised fennel, 165
        Salt cod and potato pie, 178
        Seafood soup, 78
        Shrimp and zucchini with mint pilaf, 181
    Tuna
        souvlakia with roasted pepper salad, 138
        with lentils and beans, 166
    White fish
        Baked, with saffron, leek and potatoes, 161
        Crisp, with paprika mustard butter, 154
        Crisp-skinned, with roast garlic skordalia, 157
        Grilled seafood with aioli, 170
        Lemon herb, with chickpea salad, 150
        Oven-roasted, with braised fennel, 165
        Pan-fried, with fennel and olive salad, 146
        parcels, with anchovies and olives, 162
        Roasted, with chermoulla, 169
        skewers
            Herbed, with smashed potatoes and skordalia, 142
            with tomato salad, Scallop and, 141

Spiced fried, with lemon pistachio couscous, 149
    steaks, with kalamata olive dressing, 153
    tagine, 177
flan, Cinnamon, 310
Fresh
    herb sauce, 27
    peaches and dates with orange blossom
water, 297

G

Galaktoboureko, 313
Garlic
    Baked fish with saffron, leek and potato, 161
    Braised
        borlotti beans with tomato and, 269
        chicken with chickpeas, lemon and, 22
    Cauliflower with, chilies and anchovies, 118
    Cheese and tomato tortilla, 290
    Chickpea, and mint soup, 74
    Galaktoboureko, 313
    Honeyed lamb shanks, 256
    Lamb kefta, 248
    Lemon thyme and chili marinade, 230
    mayonnaise, 205
    Moussaka, 240
    Mussels with tomato and chili, 193
    roasted, Cream of, and potato soup, 70
    Roasted pepper salad, 138
    Rosemary oil, 157
    Saffron cinnamon couscous, 130
    Shrimp, 189
    skordalia, Roast, 157
    Slow-cooked potatoes with wine and herbs, 122
    Stuffed eggplant with lamb and rice, 151
    Sweet and spicy vegetable tagine, 278
    Veal, quince and caramelized onion tagine, 244
    Vegetable tagine, 274
    Winter soup with oxtail and chickpeas, 86
Ginger
    Chicken tagine with figs and walnuts, 221
    Honeyed orange quails, 229
    Sweet and spicy vegetable tagine, 278
    Veal, quince and caramelized onion tagine, 244
    White beans and lentils, 281

Goat cheese, *see* Cheese(s)
Grape leaves
    Dolmades, 43
Greek chicken and vegetable soup, 81
Green bean(s), *see* Bean(s)
Green onion aioli, 190
Grilled
    chicken with Spanish rice, 217
    lemon thyme chicken, 226
    salmon
        with chermoulla sauce, 173
        with pepper and olive salsa, 174
    seafood with aioli, 170

H
Harissa
    Chermoulla chicken with onion
        couscous, 209
    dressing, 129
    mayonnaise, 214
    Spicy fried potatoes, 121
    White beans and lentils, 281
herb sauce, Fresh, 27
Herbed fish skewers with smashed
    potatoes and skordalia, 142
Honey
    Almond turron, 345
    Baklava, 321
    cake, Pistachio, 337
    Chicken tagine with figs and walnuts,
        221
    citrus syrup, 314
    Figs in orange syrup with yogurt
        cream, 302
    glaze, Orange, 263
    Hazelnut and date tart, 326
    lemon dressing, 90
    Spiced syrup, 318
    -spiced carrots and sweet potatoes,
        126
    Sweet and spicy vegetable tagine,
        278
    Tuna with lentils and beans, 166
    Veal, quince and caramelized onion
        tagine, 244
    Walnut cookies, 318
Honeyed
    figs, 306
    lamb shanks, 256
    orange quails, 229

L
Lamb
    Dolmades, 43
    kebabs with yogurt and pita bread, 247
    kefta, 248
    meatballs with egg-lemon sauce, 252

Moussaka, 240
    Pastitsio
        meat sauce, 243
    Stuffed eggplant with, and rice, 251
    shanks,
        Baked, with orzo, 255
        Honeyed, 256
    shoulder, Slow-roasted spiced, 259
Leek(s)
    Baked fish with saffron, and potato,
        161
    Winter soup with oxtail and chickpeas,
        86
Lemon(s)
    Aioli, 170
    and herb fish with chickpea salad, 150
    Apricot filling, 325
    Artichokes in oregano vinaigrette, 109
    Baklava syrup, 321
    Beef
        kebabs with roasted vegetable
            salad, 236
        kefta with green onion couscous,
            239
    Braised chicken with chickpeas,
        and garlic, 222
    Cauliflower with garlic, chilies and
        anchovies, 118
    Chermoulla, 209
        shrimp skewers, 186
    Cheery spoon sweet, 301
    Chicken
        and chorizo salad with garlic
            mayonnaise, 205
        and rice soup, 82
        kebabs with harissa mayonnaise,
            214
        with olives and couscous, 210
    cilantro dressing, 182
    couscous, 274
    dressing, 94
        Honey, 90
        Minted, 181
    feta toast, 73
    Garlic
        mayonnaise, 205
        shrimp, 189
    Grilled chicken
        lemon thyme, 226
        with Spanish rice, 217
        with tomato salad, 201
    Grilled seafood with aioli, 170
    Harissa
        dressing, 129
        mayonnaise, 214
    Hazelnut and date tart, 326
    Honey citrus syrup, 314

Lamb meatballs with egg-lemon
        sauce, 252
    Onion couscous, 209
    Oven-roasted fish with braised fennel,
        165
    Paprika pork chops with carrot and
        olive salad, 260
    Pistachio
        couscous, Spiced fried fish with,
            149
        honey cake, 337
    Rice pudding with cinnamon and
        vanilla, 305
    Roast garlic skordalia, 157
    Salt-baked whole snapper with fennel
        and mint salad, 158
    Shrimp souvlakia with tomato and
        fennel sauce, 185
    Slow-cooked potatoes with wine and
        herbs, 122
    Spiced syrup, 318
    syrup, 313, 333
    Thyme and garlic marinated olives, 16
    Vegetable paella, 286
Lemon thyme
    and chili marinade, 230
    and chili roast chicken, 230
    chicken, Grilled, 226
Lentil(s)
    salsa, Chicken with, 198
    soup, 66
    Tuna with, and beans, 166
    White beans and, 281
Lime(s)
    Chicken with lentil salsa, 198
Loukoumades, 314

M
Marjoram
    vinaigrette, Roasted eggplant with,
        102
Mayonnaise
    Aioli, 170
        Green onion, 190
    Garlic, 205
    Harissa, 214
Meatballs in tomato sauce, 60
Melon salad with citrus sugar, 298
Mini chicken souvlaki, 55
Mint
    Beef kefta with green onion couscous,
        239
    Carrot, raisin and herb salad, 105
    Chermoulla shrimp skewers, 186
    Chickpea, garlic and, soup, 73
    Chicken phyllo pie, 233
    Dolmades, 43

Harissa dressing, 129
Lemon pistachio couscous, 149
Mini chicken souvlaki, 55
Radish and herb salad, 106
Roasted tomato salad, 289
salad, Fennel and, 158
Shrimp souvlakia with tomato and
    fennel sauce, 185
Spinach, feta and pine nut salad, 94
Sweet cucumber and orange salad,
    90
tea, 346
Tomato
    and fennel sauce, 185
    salad, 201
Valencian salad, 93
White beans and lentils, 281
Minted
    lemon dressing, 181
    yogurt
        Fava bean patties with, 23
Moist carrot and apple cake, 338
Moroccan-style vegetables, 285
Moussaka, 240
Mushroom(s)
    Chicken in red wine and tomato
        sauce, 225
    Vegetable paella, 286
Mussels with tomato and chili, 193

N
Nut(s)
    Almond(s)
        about: flavors and varieties, 10
        Apricot jam tart, 325
        Chicken
            and chorizo salad with garlic
                mayonnaise, 205
            tagine with dried plums, 218
        Chocolate and orange polenta
            cake, 341
        Fig galettes, 322
        Orange shortbread cookies, 317
        Romesco sauce, 59
        Saffron cinnamon couscous, 130
        sauce, 206
        Stuffed peppers, 289
        Sweet and spicy vegetable tagine,
            278
        turron, 345
        Yogurt cake, 334
    Hazelnut(s)
        and date tart, 326
    Pistachio(s)
        Baklava, 321
        couscous, Lemon, 149
        dukkah

Chicken kebabs with harissa
    mayonnaise, 214
honey cake, 337
Fish tagine, 177
Orange shortbread cookies, 317
Walnut(s)
    Baklava, 321
    cake, 330
    Chicken tagine with figs and, 221
    cookies, Honey, 318
    Date nut balls, 342
    Rice pudding with cinnamon and
        vanilla, 305
    sauce, Green beans with tomato,
        113

O
Olive(s)
    about: ripeness, textures and
        varieties, 10
    Black
        and cheese fritters, 19
        Carrot and, salad, 260
    Fish parcels with anchovies and,
        162
        Pan-fried fish with fennel and,
            salad, 146
        Valencian salad, 93
    Green
        and bell peppers brown rice, 134
        butter, 202
        Chicken
            and chorizo salad with garlic
                mayonnaise, 205
            with, and couscous, 210
        Oven-roasted fish with braised
            fennel, 165
        salsa, 174
        Spanish rice, 217
    Kalamata
        dressing, 153
        Slow-cooked potatoes with wine
            and herbs, 122
        Thyme and garlic marinated, 16
Olive oil cake, 329
Onion(s)
    Artichokes, in oregano vinaigrette,
        109
    Baked cabbage with tomatoes, 114
    Beef
        and fig cigars, 56
        kebabs with roasted vegetable
            salad, 236
        kefta with green, couscous, 239
    Braised
        chicken with chickpeas, lemon and
            garlic, 222

green beans, 273
Chermoulla, 209
    dressing, 110
Chicken
    and chorizo salad with garlic
        mayonnaise, 205
    in red wine and tomato sauce, 225
    lemon and rice soup, 82
    phyllo pie, 233
    tagine with figs and walnuts, 221
    with almond sauce, 206
    with olives and couscous, 210
Chickpea
    garlic and mint soup, 74
    patties with tahini sauce, 20
    tomato stew, 77
Chili tomato salsa, 63
Chorizo and potato tortilla, 125
Clams with white wine and tomatoes,
    194
couscous, Lemon pistachio, 149
Cream
    of roasted garlic and potato soup,
        70
    of spinach soup with lemon feta
        toast, 73
    Crisp fish with paprika mustard
        butter, 154
Dolmades, 43
Eggplant, tomato and chickpea
    casserole, 266
Fava bean patties with minted yogurt,
    23
Goat cheese with chickpeas and
    bell peppers, 40
Greek chicken and vegetable soup,
    81
Green, see Scallion(s)
Grilled salmon with chermoulla sauce,
    173
Honeyed lamb shanks, 256
Kalamata olive dressing, 153
Lamb
    kebabs with yogurt and pita bread,
        247
    kefta, 248
    meatballs with egg-lemon sauce,
        252
Lentil soup, 66
Meatballs in tomato sauce
Moroccan-style vegetables, 285
Moussaka, 240
Oven-roasted fish with braised fennel,
    165
Paella croquettes, 24
Pastitsio
    Meat sauce, 243

Roasted eggplant with marjoram vinaigrette, 102
Saffron cinnamon couscous, 130
Saganaki shrimp, 52
Salt cod and potato pie, 178
Seafood soup, 78
Shredded beef soup, 85
Shrimp and zucchini with mint pilaf, 181
Slow-cooked potatoes with wine and herbs, 122
Slow-roasted spiced lamb shoulder, 259
Spiced cauliflower couscous, 117
Spiced meatballs with romesco sauce, 59
Spicy chicken and rice, 213
Spicy couscous, 129
Spicy lentil and rice salad, 277
Stuffed eggplant with lamb and rice, 251
Stuffed peppers, 289
Sweet and spicy vegetable tagine, 278
Tomato and fennel sauce, 185
Turnip soup, 69
Valencian salad, 93
Veal, quince, and caramelized, tagine, 244
Vegetable
    paella, 286
    tagine, 274
White beans and lentils, 281
Orange(s)
    blossom water, Fresh peaches and dates with, 297
    Carrot, raisin and herb salad, 105
    Chicken and almond sauce, 206
    dressing, 93
    Honey
        citrus syrup, 314
        glaze, 263
        walnut cookies, 318
    Hot chocolate, 349
    Melon salad with citrus sugar, 298
    Moist carrot and apple cake, 338
    Olive oil cake, 329
    polenta cake, Chocolate and, 341
    quails, Honeyed, 229
    salad,
        Sweet cucumber and, 90
    shortbread cookies, 317
    Spiced, with brown sugar toffee, 294
    syrup,
        Figs in, with yogurt cream, 302
    Valencian salad, 93
    Walnut cake, 330

Oregano
    Baked lamb shanks with orzo, 255
    Braised borlotti beans with tomato and garlic, 269
    Chickpea patties with tahini sauce, 20
    Deep-fried calamari, 51
    Eggplant, tomato and chickpea casserole, 266
    Feta and artichoke pizzetta, 47
    Grilled chicken
        with Spanish rice, 217
        with tomato salad, 201
    Kalamata olive dressing, 153
    Lemon dressing, 94
    Olive and bell peppers brown rice, 34
    Roasted pepper salad, 138
    Saganaki shrimp, 52
    Shredded beef soup, 85
    Stuffed eggplant with lamb and rice, 251
    Tomato and feta toasts, 32
    Tomato salad, 201
    vinaigrette, Artichokes in, 109
Orzo
    Baked lamb shanks with, 255
Ouzo
    Tomato and fennel sauce, 185
Oven-roasted fish with braised fennel, 165

P
Paella
    croquettes, 24
    Vegetable, 286
Pan-fried fish with fennel and olive salad, 146
Paprika
    mustard butter, 154
    pork chops with carrot and olive salad, 260
Parsley dressing, 101
Parsnip(s)
    Sweet and spicy vegetable tagine, 278
Pastitsio, 243
Pea(s)
    Vegetable paella, 286
Peach(es)
    Fresh, and dates with orange blossom water, 297
Phyllo pastry
    Baklava, 321
    Beef and fig cigars, 56
    Cheese, triangles, 44
    Chicken, pie, 233
    Galaktoboureko, 313
Pickled zucchini salad, 89

Pickling liquid, 89
Pineapple
    Melon salad with citrus sugar, 298
Pine nut(s)
    Beef kebabs with green onion couscous, 239
    Dolmades, 43
    Moist carrot and apple cake, 338
    Spicy couscous, 128
    Spinach, feta and pine nut salad, 94
Pita, see Bread(s)
Plum(s)
    dried, Chicken tagine with, 218
    sauce
        Beef and fig cigars, 56
Polenta
    Cake, Chocolate and orange, 341
Pork
    Chops
        with carrot and olive salad, Paprika, 260
    Ground
        Meatballs in tomato sauce, 60
    Tenderloin
        skewers, with orange honey glaze, Spiced, 263
Potato(es)
    Baked fish with saffron, leek and, 161
    Braised green beans, 273
    Chorizo and, tortilla, 125
    Cream
        of roasted garlic and, soup, 70
        of spinach soup with lemon feta toast, 73
    Greek chicken and vegetable soup, 81
    Grilled
        chicken with green olive butter, 202
        lemon thyme chicken, 226
    Herbed fish skewers with smashed potatoes and skordalia, 142
    pie, Salt cod and, 178
    Seafood soup, 78
    Skordalia, 31, 142
        Roast garlic, 157
    Slow-cooked, with wine and herbs, 122
    Spicy fried, 121
    Sweet
        Honey-spiced carrots and, 126
        Honeyed lamb shanks, 256
        Sweet and spicy vegetable tagine, 278
        tortilla, Chorizo and, 125
Puff pastry
    Fig galettes, 322

Q

Quince(s)
Veal, and caramelized onion tagine, 244

R

Radish(es)
and herb salad, 106
Raisin(s)
Apricot filling, 325
Carrot, and herb salad, 105
Chickpea tomato stew, 77
Date nut balls, 342
Fish tagine, 177
Sweet and spicy vegetable tagine, 278
Rice
Chicken
Spicy, and, 213
Lemon and rice, soup, 82
Dolmades, 43
Olive and bell peppers brown, 134
Paella croquettes, 24
pudding with cinnamon and vanilla, 305
Saffron, with zucchini flowers, 133
Salt cod and potato pie, 178
Shrimp and zucchini with mint pilaf, 181
Spanish, 217
Spicy lentil and rice salad, 277
Stuffed
eggplant with lamb and, 251
peppers, 289
Vegetable paella, 286
Roasted eggplant with marjoram vinaigrette, 102
Roasted pepper salad, 138
Roasted white fish with chermoulla, 169
Romesco sauce, 59
Rosemary oil, 157

S

Saffron
cinnamon couscous, 130
leek and potato, Baked fish with, 161
panna cotta with honeyed figs, 306
rice with zucchini flowers, 133
Saganaki shrimp, 52
Salt cod and potato pie, 178
Salt-baked whole snapper with fennel and mint salad, 158
Sardine(s), *see* Fish
Scallion(s)
Cheese and tomato tortilla, 290

Chorizo
and potato tortilla, 125
cones with salsa, 63
Clams with white wine and tomatoes, 194
Green onion aioli, 190
Spanish rice, 217
Spicy lentil and rice salad, 277
Tomato salad, 201
Scallop(s)
and fish skewers with tomato salad, 141
Seafood
Grilled, with aioli, 170
soup, 78
Semolina
Baklava, 321
Galaktoboureko, 313
Honey walnut cookies, 318
Sesame cream, 326
Shallot(s)
Chicken tagine with dried plums, 218
Grilled lemon thyme chicken, 226
Mussels with tomato and chili, 193
Sardine dip, 28
Vegetable kebabs, 282
Shredded beef soup, 85
Shrimp
and couscous salad with lemon cilantro dressing, 182
and zucchini with mint pilaf, 181
Garlic, 189
Grilled seafood with aioli, 170
Saganaki, 52
skewers, Chermoulla, 186
souvlakia with tomato and fennel sauce, 185
Skordalia, 31, 142
Roast garlic, 157
Slow-cooked potatoes with wine and herbs, 122
Slow-roasted spiced lamb shoulder, 259
Soft shell crabs with green onion aioli, 190
Spiced
cauliflower couscous, 117
coffee with rosewatercream, 350
crème caramel, 309
fried fish with lemon pistachio couscous, 149
meatballs with romesco sauce, 59
oranges with brown sugar toffee, 294

pork skewers with orange honey glaze, 263
syrup, 318
Spicy
couscous, 129
fried potatoes, 121
lentil and rice salad, 277
Spinach
Chicken tagine with figs and walnuts, 221
Chickpea tomato stew, 77
Crisp fish with paprika mustard butter, 154
dip, Artichoke, 35
feta and pine nut salad, 94
Lamb meatballs with egg-lemon sauce, 252
soup, Cream of, with lemon feta toast, 73
Split pea(s)
Fava bean patties with minted yogurt, 23
Squash
Sweet and spicy vegetable tagine, 278
Vegetable tagine, 274
Stuffed
eggplant with lamb and rice, 251
peppers, 289
Sweet
and spicy vegetable tagine, 278
cucumber and orange salad, 90
Swiss chard
Braised green beans, 273

T

Tagine(s)
Chicken
with dried plums, 218
with figs and walnuts, 221
Fish, 177
Sweet and spicy vegetable, 278
Veal, quince and caramelized onion, 244
Vegetable, 274
Tahini
sauce, Chickpea patties with, 20
Thyme
and garlic marinated olives, 16
Cream of roasted garlic and potato soup, 70
Herbed fish skewers with smashed potatoes and skordalia, 142
Tomato(es)
and fennel sauce, 185
and feta toasts, 32

and herb salad, 98
Baked lamb shanks with orzo, 255
Beef kebabs with roasted vegetable
    salad, 236
Baked cabbage with, 114
Braised
    borlotti beans with, and garlic, 269
    green beans, 273
Chickpea
    garlic and mint soup, 74
    tomato stew, 77
Clams with white wine and, 194
Crisp fish with paprika mustard butter,
    154
dressing, 270
    and herb salad, 98
Eggplant
    and chickpea casserole, 266
    dip, 36
Greek chicken and vegetable soup,
    81
Lamb kefta, 248
Lentil soup, 66
Moroccan-style vegetables, 285
Moussaka, 240
Mussels with, and chili, 193
Olive salsa, 174
Pastitsio
    meat sauce, 243
Radish and herb salad, 106
Romesco sauce, 243
Saganaki shrimp, 52
salad, 201
    Roasted, 289
    Scallop and fish skewers with, 141
salsa, Chili, 63
sauce
    Chicken in red wine and, 225
    Meatballs in, 60
Seafood soup, 78
Shredded beef soup, 85
Spicy chicken and rice, 213
Stuffed peppers, 289
Sweet and spicy vegetable tagine, 278
tortilla, Cheese and, 290
Valencian salad, 93
Vegetable

kebabs, 282
    tagine, 274
walnut sauce, Green beans with, 113
White beans and lentils, 281
Tortilla(s)
    Cheese and tomato, 290
    Chorizo
        and potato, 125
        cones with salsa, 63
        Shredded beef soup, 85
Turnip soup, 69

V
Valencian salad, 93
Veal, quince and caramelized onion
    tagine, 244
Vegetable
    kebabs, 282
    paella, 286
    stock
        Chickpea tomato stew, 77
        Moroccan-style vegetables, 285
        tagine, 274
            Sweet and spicy, 278

W
Walnut(s), see Nut(s)
Watercress
    Shrimp and couscous salad with
        lemon cilantro dressing, 182
Watermelon
    Melon salad with citrus sugar, 298
White bean dip with pita crisps, 39
White beans and lentils, 281
White sauce, 240
Wine
    Red
        Chicken in, and tomato sauce, 225
        Date nut balls, 342
        Honeyed
            figs, 306
            lamb shanks, 256
        Spicy chicken and rice, 213
        vinaigrette, 134, 141
    White
        Almond sauce, 206
        Clams with, and tomatoes, 194

Fish tagine, 177
Garlic shrimp, 189
Mussels with tomato sauce, 193
Oven-roasted fish with braised
    fennel, 165
Moussaka, 240
Pastitsio, 234
Saganaki shrimp, 52
Seafood soup, 78
Slow-cooked potatoes with, and
    herbs, 122
Shrimp and zucchini with mint pilaf,
    181
Winter soup with oxtail and chickpeas,
    86

Y
Yogurt
    cake, 334
    Dolmades, 43
    Greek style Chermoulla sauce, 173
        Fresh peaches and dates with
            orange blossom water, 297
        Skordalia, Roast, 157
    Lamb kebabs with, and pita bread,
        247
    Minted
        Fava bean patties with, 23

Z
Za'atar
    about: blend of spices, 13
Zucchini
    Fennel and mint salad, 158
    Greek chicken and vegetable soup,
        81
    Grilled
        salmon with chermoulla sauce, 173
        seafood with aioli, 170
    Moroccan-style vegetables, 285
    Saffron rice with, 133
    salad, Pickled, 89
    Shrimp and, with mint pilaf, 181
    with chermoulla dressing, 110
    Vegetable kebabs, 282

STERLING
New York

An Imprint of Sterling Publishing
387 Park Avenue South
New York, NY 10016

ISBN 978-1-4549-1188-3

Distributed in Canada by Sterling Publishing
c/o Canadian Manda Group, 165 Dufferin Street
Toronto, Ontario, Canada M6K 3H6

For information about custom editions, special sales, and premium and corporate purchases,
please contact Sterling Special Sales at 800-805-5489 or specialsales@sterlingpublishing.com.

Manufactured in the China

2 4 6 8 10 9 7 5 3 1

www.sterlingpublishing.com